For Bill,
with my sincere
appreciation of all that y[ou]
With Love Cla[...]

Gifts
from the
EDGE

Stories of the Other Side

CLAUDIA WATTS EDGE

GIFTS FROM THE EDGE
Stories of the Other Side

ISBN-13: 978-0-692-94185-0
ISBN-10: 0-692-94185-1

Library of Congress Control Number: 2018900263

Retail, Wholesale, Bookstores, Libraries, Academic:
eStore www.amazon.com/dp/0692941851
Printed by CreateSpace, An Amazon.com Company

Cover image: "Tourist in Mountains" ID 62117594 © Dmitry Islentyev, release Dreamstime, standard license.

Cover Design & Illustration: Curtis Pearson, CPImagingdesign.com

Web: ClaudiaEdge.com
Facebook: www.facebook.com/claudiawattsedge

Dedication

~~~

I dedicate this book to the children, for they are our best and brightest hopes for future change.

Especially to my grandchildren, Andrew Clayton Locher, Ava Anderson, Jude Clayton, Addison Clayton, Zoe Anderson, Jaydan Coulson, Harper Coulson, Violet Gaskins, Jessica and Marcos Deherrera, Joey Medina, Vanessa and Ryan Deherrera, and Sawyer Clayton.

One can only guess at the wonder of becoming a grandparent. I feel it is akin to what is awaiting us on the Other Side in unconditional love. I find blissful joy in hearing these little ones call me Grandma. It is the sweetest sound I have ever heard and the greatest job I have ever had.

— CLAUDIA WATTS CLAYTON EDGE

~~~

Reviews

~

"Inspiring – and inspired! Claudia has a rare and beautiful gift. She hears and sees loved ones on the Other Side. Through her eloquent writing, the kindness of her soul shines through and we are graced with insights and visions of life beyond this one. This splendid book is a true legacy, for all of us who are blessed to have found this little gem of a book. Written with grace and humility, yet a delightful sense of humor, Gifts from the Edge is a treasure. A book to cherish! For all souls, young and old."

~

Charol Messenger,
Author of inspirational books, including
"You 2.0" and "The Soul Path"

~

"Gifts from the Edge - Stories from the Other Side", by Claudia Watts Edge Is a poignant retrospective of personal memories, visions and dreams that will tug at your heart strings and inspire you. Reminding us our love is eternal."

— Mary Deioma, author of
"Loved: A Transcendent Journey"

~

"Claudia Watts Edge had a dream to communicate and in her book Gifts from the Edge: Stories of the Other Side she has fulfilled her dream. Claudia shares her visions, dreams, memories, and messages from the other side in a style that makes this memoir touch your heart in a very special way. Filled with her spiritual insights you'll find it moving and see how it makes you aware that there are divine messages in all of our daily interactions."

— David Bennett,
Author of "Voyage of Purpose" & "A Voice as Old as Time"
DharmaTalks.com

~

About The Author

Claudia Watts Clayton Edge is a happily married mother of five children, three stepdaughters and nine grandchildren, and is a working realtor in Salt Lake City, Utah.

During the birth of her last child she had a near death experience, leaving a slow residual effect that took nearly thirty years to fully surface. Feeling a purpose to what she could remember from The Beyond, Claudia worked toward regaining full cognizance of her NDE.

She has spent the entirety of her life since then focused on all aspects of research into life after life phenomena, driven by her curiosity, openness, and acceptance of new ideas in her relentless search for answers and a deeper understanding.

This personal memoir embodies Claudia's recollections of her spiritual awakening to soul enlightenment and advancement in the pathway to communication with the Other Side, both visually and auditorily, which she has humbly worked to enhance.

She has been writing stories of the Afterlife for many years, including her first book at the age of sixteen, as her own personal beliefs and strength of knowing that communication with those who have passed is entirely possible. Claudia reveals through stories that our loved ones are willing and able to show much more than we know about life—only if we ask.

Claudia spent five years in volunteer hospice service in Colorado Springs, Colorado, practicing three of those years on "the bridge" (between worlds) at Pikes Peak hospital. She has also worked as a volunteer for the AFSP American Foundation for Suicide Prevention. She is a full time real estate agent, but her favorite title is Grandma.

Preface

A few words from the author...

~ ~ ~

Fractured Fairy Tales

Dearest readers:

Many of you grew up with, or are familiar with the *Rocky and Bullwinkle* television show, a Saturday morning cartoon series of animated stories. One segment was called "Fractured Fairy Tales." In the opening, a flying fairy dressed in fluffy pink princess splendor with a huge pointed hat, points a magic wand at a large fancy book that is hanging effortlessly in the air.

Last night, I had a dream experience containing this cartoon. The fairy was very memorable, because she made every effort to keep my attention. *"Yes, I am paying attention,"* I said to her as she continued, turning toward me.

Then she touched the book with her wand and the pages began to turn. She turned to me again. *"Yes, I am still paying attention,"* I said as I nodded.

From the tip of her wand, she turned another page, and then turned to me yet again to see if I was still watching. *"Yes, I am watching."* I said. By now, I definitely was.

I don't recall the title of the book or the writings on the first few pages. But one page stuck out to me and has stayed with me.

The fairy was pointing to a blank white page in the fancy floating book, when words in fancy calligraphy and shining stars came forth from the wand's tip and scrolled across the page:

Talk to Your Family

The message was clear, and I was definitely paying attention.

~ ~ ~

I have thought of these words often since the dream, because I had thought I was doing a pretty good job of staying in contact with my family and I didn't think I had a problem in my communication with them.

Nevertheless, I took these words from the dream literally, and in the next few days called or visited my family.

"It has now been several years since this highly visual dream, and I learned much in the interpretation of such dreams, each one playing an intricate part in my expanding awareness. I have allowed myself to be open and ready for new concepts to be introduced. I have also learned much about the guide who has stayed near me during these learning years. I lovingly call him Click Click, and he is OK with it, because his name is difficult to replicate in human language. I have found that the more I communicate with him, the more he communicates back. Funny how that happens, a true friendship has developed between us.

He has taught me how to pay attention during my dreams. One surefire way has been to wear outrageous costumes, as I learned that he was also the beautiful fairy princess in the beginning of my lessons. He works very hard to get my attention and to spark my cognizance while dreaming, so I wake up later with an improved ability to recall the message he brings.

I laugh aloud at some of the get-ups he has dawned on my behalf, he has posed as Mrs. Doubtfire, the Lady in Red, a Whirling Dervish, and he has even shown up in a bow tie and neatly pressed uniform of the Texaco man from the 1960's, a quick salute and he's ready for gas station service. This is only a smattering of the lengths he will go to wake me up so to speak, to become lucid enough within my dreams to remember them, and also gives me something to giggle about later.

He has proven to be there for me, even before I understood how this could even be possible, and through his messages, attached with intended comedic relief, he has given me a hand up in accepting that my psychic dreams and stories needed to be put together in a book. It started with the vision I had of him, wearing a serious expression and a brown hooded robe, holding a computer and pushing it toward me, saying, *"Like Nostradamus, Socrates and Plato, your dreams matter."* He did not mince words here, and I listened. I have prayed and meditated on what materials would be appropriate to include in this book, because the thought of outing myself as being 'different' was very difficult in the beginning.

Nevertheless, I was encouraged—*delicately pushed*—by the words I had been given, like, *"The words given are yours to use"* and *"The courage you seek is inside of you to step onto the world stage."* Even *"Organize your original notes"* when I was in the midst of trying to edit my dream journals, then in a dream I was *shown* how the book could be put together.

So here I sit and type with the intent of sharing the dreams and visions I have received. I have been nudged, pushed, inspired, and outright told to share the messages in my dreams, because they contain valuable lessons gifted from the Other Side.

I have no expectations of how this collection of stories about my dreams and visions will be received by my family or my world family. I am only humbled and honored by a higher power that believes in my ability to string the words together with sincere emotion into a readable and hopefully enjoyable form of expression.

Stories are the way our ancestors have shared lessons since the beginning of time, woven into story form and told by great tellers around campfires, later written into books. These are the ways to bring home the beautiful teachings from beyond the veil of God/Source, our Guides, and Angel Teachers.

Many of my dreams contained a clear heading as *METAPHOR*, a symbolic idea, word or phrase representing the dream's message so it would be easier for me to grasp and comprehend, especially abstract concepts that were new to me, so I would have no doubt what I was being shown was a teaching story from the Infinite.

It is my personal belief that many of the books we cherish were translated without these types of headings. Many of the dreams offered to seers in the past were shown as teaching stories to be shared and were not meant to be worshiped or to have entire belief systems built around them; they were not meant to be taken literally but only as inspiration, to gently steer answers to people's questions, like, "Why am I here? Am I on the right path?"

I write the disclaimer as instructed by a higher power, so this will not mistakenly happen again.

I offer the stories in this book as living breathing lessons, to be read and incorporated as such.

This is how I offer this book, dear reader, whoever you are. I do not tout myself as an advanced or gifted soul, only someone with a questioning mind of the before-and-after life. I have an incessant craving to study, learn, and experience, and then share the indelible KNOWING that has followed me since childhood.

I have learned that *yes*, there is more. Before, I didn't really know what, but I always *knew* there was more, that there just had to be, and I wanted to find out what that intangible *something more* is. This was and is my continued quest, to receive firsthand knowledge then share what I learn.

This book contains the questions - the beginnings of my personal quest, and the gradual confidence I gleaned as real answers were received. It contains the growth and awareness of my own spiritual journey and awakening, supported by my near-death experience and my sixty-plus years of life experience that has offered personal growth. I have worked very hard to advance my auditory and visual abilities, opening a pathway to communication with the Other Side.

These psychic gifts are held by all of us and are ours to cultivate and use. We were not sent here without a support system. However, accessing and using these abilities must be truly desired and indeed asked for, because the greatest gift given to us is our *free will*, which we can use to explore the unknown or to live in the manner of our own choosing. There is no judgment in the choice, only a grand and universal support system to all who are curious and *ask* for assistance.

Many signs, dreams, books, and people have *shown up* in my life at the exact times I needed them. I have lovingly named them my stones, each creating a new step along my path to enlightenment. I have not traveled this earthly journey unaided. Nor do any of us. I am grateful for all that have helped me along the way.

I am grateful for my own curiosity, ignited by the death of my beloved father when I was sixteen. His loss impacted me deeply and was the catalyst of my lifelong unquenchable thirst for knowledge of where all the beautiful loving energy that was him had gone and, through this search came answers to what comes *before* this life as well as *after we* leave this world.

Having been driven my entire life to go beyond the simple acceptance of belief and faith, I have worked for a personal relationship with God, always believing that somehow I am worthy of it, with no middleman needed to achieve this goal. I mean no disrespect to any religion, because I believe all are important for our growth and support of cultural likeness and acceptance. I only speak of my own deep-seated hunger for more answers than what I was being given. As a rebel, I needed space for my own decision-making, because I just knew that God's world contained a full spectrum of colors and I could not find myself following strict teachings of a black or white/good or bad construct.

I pray that the incidents and dreams written in the following pages enhance or motivate your own quest to *know,* to search, to read, and to find the wonder through digging deeper; to begin your own dialogue with a loved one who has passed beyond your sight, then look for and expect to be answered back; and to kindle communication and a precious friendship with your guides, for they are your loving companions in this world, with whom you will never be alone.

~ ~ ~

Well-Placed Stones

The stories, dream-experiences and visions in this book came directly from my journals. In deeply personal and private pages, I record the wonderful things I see, hear, feel, and dream.

Within these pages, I have tried to capture the essence of my very soul. With the guidance of a loving presence, I have been shown the breadth of my soul's journey through time, a gift I have generously been given from which to learn, grow and explore the depths of who I truly am.

Since going through the veil of amnesia upon this birth as Claudia, it has taken a deep inner searching and also a personal letting go of old taught belief systems and allowing myself the chance to rediscover an underlying feeling into a confident knowing—remembering—of the wonders that await us on the Other Side.

This letting go has occurred, for me, in baby steps, as new research materials suddenly show up, a new theory or something I remember after an intense dream. I think deeply about the new idea at first, giving it some time to settle, then I hold it up to the light and look at it carefully, with a discerning eye. If it holds the light and continues to resonate with me, I will allow the knowledge in, to be digested and to meld into and become a part of me and who I am, and what I know to be true.

I have prayed and asked the Universe for help in so many different ways. With the loving help of the many who have been "placed" before me on my path—I have long called them The Stones Along The Road, people who became instant friends and books that just happened to appear at the right time—Stepping Stones of Assistance in my great need to know. All of this grew from a seedling of curiosity.

What I am saying is, answers do come when asked for. The Universe happily offers the answers we seek, but they do have to be truly desired and asked for, because our free will trumps everything else in our experience here.

I have been making a conscious effort, to notice the subtle ways we are gently nudged. Surprising to me, this book has grown into something much bigger than my original intention. What I was going to share from my personal journal pages? How deep would I go? How would these stories of visions and dreams be received? Would my friends and family see me differently? They might think I've "cracked" and, in a way, they would be right—because in order to let something new in, there has to be an opening.

I have visualized mine. It is at the top of my head, and the crack can be seen by those who are on the Other Side. If they are looking, they might notice someone here who is wishing and willing to communicate. They would also see *me* as someone ready to let some old unused ideas out; and more importantly, will bravely allow some new ideas in.

The invisible crack at the crown of my head is now one of my greatest sources of pride. Yes, I know now it is the crown chakra, and it is important to note here that we all have one. I am just now noticing that mine has definitely opened and is receiving. I humbly offer these stories in the hope of adding to your own personal beliefs and to the strength of your own *knowing*.

I also now consider my emotional sensitivity, my "tender feelings" as they have been called, as strength. This something so tease-worthy in my youth is *now* my mantle and I wear it with pride, as it is a part of who I am.

~ Most sincerely,
Claudia Edge, Seeker

Foreword

~ ~ ~

Daring to Dream

"*I am supposed to know you*" came this bold statement from a woman who vaguely caught the corner of my eye as I dashed past her in my large antique emporium. *"Are you Deirdre?"* It was a hectic Saturday and I was busily helping a customer out the door with her purchases. My initial reaction was *Huh? Did she just say that to me? Who approaches someone and starts off conversing in that way*?

Apparently, it was my soon to be dear friend—a person with whom I would forge a strong bond and a loving connection, that's who. She had seen me on a the recent TV program called "*I Survived Death—Beyond and Back.*" I was speaking about my Near Death Experience. Feeling (and rightfully so) that we were somehow kindred spirits, once she found out I lived in a town not far from hers she set out to find me. That is how Claudia Edge operates...not necessarily or always by logic, reason, or even by the seat of her pants - *but* by her intuition and her heart. She speaks her truth with it as well.

So meet one another we did. As she and I began to grow in our friendship we shared and exchanged life stories. We exchanged our inner hopes, difficulties, ambitions, and desires. We also shared our dreams. Not just daydream type of thoughts but real dreams and what they might mean to each. Most of *my* dreams, which have been sporadic at best, are usually fragmented, nonsensical. More often than not they have no real thread or story line. Trying to discover what they might mean or what lessons they carry has almost always been beyond my ability to definitively figure out. Claudia however, is naturally quite gifted in the dream department. Though fanciful or sometimes bizarre in their presentations they always seem to have a beginning, middle and an end. *AND,* they have quite the life lessons to give or reveal to her in the process. I will have to say that I have certainly acquired "dream envy" from this one who so willingly delves head on into slumber and tackles with gusto the lessons given her in "Spirit School."

For many, dreams are the place to go to escape the bonds of daytime living. Some dream, while others seem or claim not to dream at all. Some dream in color, others in black and white. Sometimes beautiful, illogical, or even frightening dreams can be just that—an escape into another world. Many of us don't remember with any great regularity what the nighttime theater has acted out upon our stage of sleep. These mixed up snippets of dream-world events or actions fade out with the morning light. Vague wispy fragments may stay for a bit to replay themselves in front of our mind's eyes but are quick to dissolve as the daytime world once again takes center stage.

In this truly captivating book Claudia now takes us with her on a journey into the realms of her inner self. She shares with readers how these dreams have touched her soul and what they might offer in the way of life lessons or answers. There are answers for not only her but also many of us who are questioning life and its amazing mysterious process. We all know we are here in the physical sense, yet we know too that the underlying essence of who we are in true form is so much more. It is in our dreams that we can embrace this being-ness on another level; and this, is where Claudia has become a true explorer.

Within many of her dreams and day-to-day intuitions she has also come to realize that there are available connections to souls who have passed on. Most are loved ones that have come to her from far beyond the earthly constraints of a bodily shell; they are in the essence of spirit. She has reached her hand across the veil where it is then taken in love by those wishing to convey words of comfort or feelings of closeness back again to our worldly domain and to those they left behind. Claudia is an open conduit for earth-to-spirit realm communication.

Join her on this journey as she gifts us with her insightfulness, her wit and loving heart all wrapped up within these pages you are about to explore. The connection between self and Creator strong within her words as is the connection she creates to us and our heartfelt desire to know and understand more about the essence and importance of being - who are we, what we are here for, and where we are going? *And, to you Claudia my dear friend, God has gifted you with many spiritual gifts, you are using them well.*

In the words of her dream world teacher...*"This one gets an A."*

~ *Deirdre DeWitt-Maltby*
Near Death Experiencer

Author of "While I Was Out"
and "This is For You (Whispers of the Soul)"

deirdremaltby.com

Contents

GIFTS FROM THE EDGE

~ ~ ~

The messages are there, if we ask for them and pay attention.
Our loved ones, who are no longer with us in the physical sense,
are so happy to help us and give us what we need.
They are near, and they are listening.

They love us always as we stumble along, encouraging us to be
more like a weed, and stop trying to conform and grow in strict rows.
Just be the beautiful and uniquely free spirit you were created to be.

And, like a dandelion dance freely in the wind.

~ ~ ~

Gifts

from the

EDGE

Stories of the **OTHER SIDE**

CLAUDIA WATTS EDGE

~ ~ ~

Before sleep, I prayed for clarity about my path in this world.
And the following words came to me in a dream...

BOOTS ON THE GROUND WHERE
CELESTIAL PAVEMENT ENDS

~ ~ ~

1

I'm still me, Just Different...

~ ~ ~

Directional Signs

Imagine suddenly finding yourself on the Other Side, having had no chance to say your goodbyes.

It is beautiful, wonderful and loving there, and you are getting used to the lighter, heavenly vibration—because you are now more than the physical body. You are a *form* of energy and light.

So, words are no longer needed to communicate. A type of telepathy is the heavenly language. It is complete and there is no room for misunderstanding. All is communicated completely through thought.

There is just one underlying issue you would really like to solve. Your sudden departure has left you wishing to communicate with those you left behind. The ones you love are still crying out for you, left in sadness and confusion, and you want to let them know you are okay, that you still exist and are feeling really great in your new digs.

The problem lies with the inability to communicate that you still exist, though now in a light and energy body, and your loved ones left behind are hindered by their heavy third-dimensional meat bodies. In the lower frequency of vibration those who remain can only understand earth's language and only *listen* with their physical mortal ears, so they can no longer *hear* you.

What can you do? How do you get a message to them?

Perhaps if you concentrate and send your love in the form of energy, a vibration that can create a *feeling* in them; something that cannot be touched, only felt, to evoke an instinct, such as an energy that raises the hair on the arm or a puff of soft warm air felt behind the ear.

For example, your loved one looks up and sees a double rainbow, or a floating feather, or a dragonfly that lands on their shoulder. Maybe there is a chance they will notice this as a sign from you—a sign that you are not gone, that you are OK and you hear them. Feeling and seeing your sign, your loved one's tears are dried and, if only momentarily, bask in the feeling of the love you are sending.

I consciously choose to live within this wonderful conclusion, and here is one of many examples why I believe that communication has been accomplished:

A Directional Signal, Keep Going—
You're Doing Great...

It was a perfect beautiful day and I was in such a good mood and really appreciating the approach of spring. I was in my car, sunroof open, taking in full deep breaths of clean sweet air.

A red light stopped me at the entrance ramp to the freeway, and my open windows were allowing the loud reverberation noise from cars on the bridge above.

"Oh, I don't want to close the windows on this perfect day," I said aloud. "I want a few more minutes of spring!"

Just as these words left my mouth, it hit me—*spring*—how could spring arrive without my sister? The tears that followed startled me, arriving so swiftly, the grief of my sister's passing still coming in unsuspecting waves.

It was a long red light as I cried and spoke her name, aloud. "Kaylyn"

I pushed my head back against the headrest and, as I did this, a thought came to mind to look to the sky for her—but there was no sky, because I was still under the bridge waiting for the light to change.

Then right above me, on the underbelly of the bridge, I noticed a worn-through spot, a pinprick really, but big enough to let in drips of water heavy with dirt and salt from the road above. In this spot, drip-by-drip, the water created a rusted image on the exposed steel. It looked like an arrow, ====> a directional mark pointing exactly the way I was headed.

There were no other marks underneath the bridge, only in this one particular spot right above my head, and I just *knew* I was looking at a message for me.

Tangible and intangible at the same time—prompted to look upward while speaking Kaylyn's name, I saw this directional sign and felt its intent and sentiment—it was Kaylyn's encouragement: *Keep going. Keep going. You're doing great. Just keep charging ahead and keep enjoying these beautiful days.*

Yes, this might have been happenstance—a grieving woman missing her younger sister, interpreting a simple marking under a bridge as communication and comfort—but what if it is real? Could it be real?

My belief in the possibility of receiving a sign from my sister was just the beginning—a series of communications began between us, as if a doorway had been opened and the feeling of separation slipped away.

My sister Kaylyn was instrumental in my forward progression of reaching into the Hereafter. Our connections and the subsequent teachings that resulted from them have only grown stronger over the years—how ironic that in the loss of her, so much has been given back to me.

~ ~ ~

~ ~ ~

"Inside of you is the courage you seek
—to step up to the world stage."

These words were given to me in a dream. They scrolled across my vision as a lifeline in a time of great angst. I was wrestling between who I thought I was and who I was meant to be.

Sometimes in desperation, our abilities can be enhanced beyond what we can imagine.

~ ~ ~

2

Contacting the Beyond

~ ~ ~

An Exchange Money Can't Buy

How helpless I felt when my son Jesse, who was living many states away, called to tell me that the second surgery for his wife Jami was causing unusual and excruciating pain. She had been through breast cancer, a double mastectomy and breast augmentation—a stretching and manipulation of the remaining skin—and now much of the precious tissue that remained was dying. Jesse had already missed so much work in these previous weeks and he wasn't easily able to leave his job, so Jami had decided not to bother him and had begun to drive herself to the hospital. Or at least she tried. Halfway there, the car broke down.

In pain, and in traffic on a busy street, Jami dropped to her knees and cried, "Mom, help me!"

Physically and mentally exhausted from so much pain and facing a third surgery in twenty days, her tears came. Like all of us in pain or fear, we want our mom—but Jami's cries were in vain, as her mother had passed several years ago.

I had to do something to help Jami get through this. I contacted a metaphysical group I trusted, to see if anyone there could give Jami a reading and reach her mother on the Other Side, for motherly words of love that Jami could hold onto.

The woman who offered to help told me the cost for her service, but at that time, I just couldn't pay what she was asking. Where could

I get the money? My thoughts were caught in a squirrel cage wheel, rolling in place over and over again. Then, plain as day, a clear voice inside my head said, *"Does the exchange of money make someone else's gift more valued than your own? Why not use your own key to open the door and get what you want?"*

"Oh, wow!" I thought, as a timid "Okay" came from my lips.

My mind continued to race. I had been able to talk with spirits, but they had come and contacted me. I was just lucky enough to *hear* it. I had never felt bold enough to ask for more than what I was given. I was grateful for the contact I had received from my sister, but I hadn't been the one to initiate it—the voice I heard had come to me. Could it be that I could make it go both ways? Could I be the one to initiate contact?

I had watched many television psychics over the years. Some are so truly gifted, born with a special channel. I would give anything to be able to do what they do, with the ease in which they do it.

It took me most of that night. It was very hard to stay in a meditative state at the higher frequency and vibration and become a bridge between both worlds—but I did it!

I asked Jami's mother to come, even though I didn't know her name. She had passed before I got a chance to know her, but I gave Jami's full name and offered my sincere intent. I continued doing this, over and over, until I felt a gentle softness in the air around me, and a presence, and I just knew it was her—*she had heard me!*

I asked if I could speak with her, mother to mother, and told her that her child was in great need and that I knew we could do this if we worked together.

I got many visuals over the next few hours, personal things only Jami would know. In respect for her privacy, I do not share them here but I wrote down everything I felt and saw.

Many times, I dropped off to sleep but was soon startled awake. I asked if she was still there—again silently, in my mind—and she was. She was right there waiting for me to come back.

I couldn't have asked for a more gracious and patient teacher. As I stumbled my way through this new territory, I felt a kinship in working with her, our goals the same. When finished, she thanked me for caring for her daughter and would I please let Jami know that she was with her and hoped she could feel her hugs.

I called Jesse the next morning and told him that I had worked very hard and had communicated with Jami's mom in the Hereafter. Although he supported me in my efforts, nothing on the list I had compiled about special nicknames, childhood pets or things they had done together resonated with him. He was unsure if what I had to share would be helpful to Jami.

I hung up the phone, trying not to feel discouraged, but self-doubt began to spin its sticky web around me. *"What was I thinking? Who was I to think I could reach Jami's deceased mother?"* If I held still too long I would be wrapped tightly into a cocoon of self-doubt and confusion—so I did not hold still. Instead I drew on the strength of what I knew to be true and used it to rise. From the depths of my soul, I knew that I had spoken to Jami's mother.

I knew the feeling of peace that her presence had brought me, and the genuine love and care that we had experienced together as she sent me the messages. I held in my hand a list from her, this *I knew to be true*. I phoned Jami, catching her awake, and she confirmed them all, one by one, things my son never knew about his wife and things only she would remember. Jami laughed as childhood memories were evoked by a single word, and she shared the details with me, filling in the blanks of things only she and her mother would know. Jami cried in her acceptance that this list of key words came directly from her mother, and she felt her mother's love coming through them.

I have learned so much in the last few years of research and personal practice, and I am happy to state with 100 percent certainty that our loved ones who have passed and transitioned are only in the next room. One of my favorite quotes is by Richard Martini, a gifted writer and film director, who writes, "They are not gone, they are just not here." The simplicity in this eloquent statement speaks volumes. They are not gone, they are just not here, and I have spent my life working to bridge the gap between here, and there.

~ ~ ~

~

Not long ago, I was soaking in a bubble bath of soothing warm water, feeling blessed as I sat in my tub next to a window overlooking my flower garden, the sun giving its golden hue, the flower heads nodding in a gentle breeze. It was Easter Sunday, and I was in gratitude on this calm morning for all the comforts I enjoy, and also of God and Jesus (Easter, you know). I outstretched my hand to touch the beautiful feeling in the room, and the following thoughts came into my mind. I jumped out of the tub to find pen and paper to capture them:

~ ~ ~

Extend your hand...

Extend your hand, but not to me, as I am always here beside you.
You have the knowledge of this to be true.
Instead, use your hands to lift up others around you,
For this is your true calling.
The knowledge you seek is already inside of you, dear teacher.
It is time to softly guide and pull forward those on unsteady step.
You, dear teacher, will sure the steps of others into enlightenment
And the knowledge of all there is.
It is time to begin.

~ ~ ~

3

Spirit School

~ ~ ~

Lesson 1:
Cause & Effect
Bingo—this one gets an A!

There are nights that I dream of being in a kind of school, sometimes outside in nature sitting on the grass and among the trees, but most of the time in a space that *feels* like a classroom. I have no recollection of ceiling or walls, or of the other students in attendance, yet I know there are others alongside me. I can *feel* their presence. The following is one of the lessons we were being taught in what I lovingly call Spirit School.

I remember being seated in a chair and facing a circle of twelve bubbles or spheres. They were rotating clockwise in front of me. Each one had a colorful luminescence, like the sun's reflection on a soap bubble revealing a rainbow, but these bubbles in front of me now held the most inexplicable colors I have ever seen.

Contained within each bubble was a hologram, a living picture. As I watched these bubbles rotating, I saw that the holograms were all reflections of *me*, showing me in this exact moment that I was sitting in this chair.

As the images rotated, I felt encouraged to do something. So, I moved my hand up to my face, flipped my hair, scrunched my nose, laughed, and stuck out my tongue. As I made these movements, the hologram inside each bubble reflected my actions. Then that bubble slipped out of rotation and drifted off, and another bubble took its place. As this continued, I felt encouraged to create different motions. As I did, each bubble removed itself from the circle and floated away—continuing to mirror the motion I had created, the hologram still active and alive.

I was fascinated while learning this lesson of cause and effect, realizing that whatever action I created caused a reaction within the bubble.

I was catching on and said to the teacher, "So the bubbles are going off into many directions and dimensions."

The teacher said, "Yes," and leaned in closer with a nod for me to continue sharing my thoughts.

So I said, "The actions we create go on living, no matter how simple or complex. The choices and decisions we make, the crossroads we stand at, all of these actions continue on and on in another dimension."

"Yes!" he said. "Good!" With that, he turned from me to address another student.

My mind was still racing with so many possibilities. *Wow!* I thought. *There must be a lot of bubbles out there from so many of us, since we are all constantly sending out these action bubbles. So there must be so many dimensions out there for all of these bubbles to go to and continue on!*

My thoughts were apparently heard by the teacher, as he now swung around and faced me with a huge smile, and one sharp clap, and then pointed directly at me and said with excitement, "Bingo! This one gets an A!"

~

Lesson 2:
Layering Description & Explanation
Describe brown.

In a dream state, I was in Spirit School again. I love Spirit School! It's the perfect environment to develop and learn. The teachers are warm and loving, and there is never any pressure of a test or a stupid question. The teacher is happy to help you learn and is genuinely excited when you grasp the concept being taught.

Tonight's class was "Description and Explanation."

The teacher handed me a small round decorative couch pillow. It was made of a translucent, see-through fabric, light brown in color, with small pink, velvet polka dots all over it. I had seen this fabric somewhere before, but probably not since the late 1950s or early 1960s.

As I looked at the pillow in my hands, the teacher said, "Describe it to me." I began, but he interrupted me halfway through my account, and said, "How would you describe it to me if you had never seen this color before?"

I thought for a moment about the color of an onion, the way all the layers converge at the top to form a color at the stem and outer shell. This would be a good explanation of the translucency, yet still forming into a color.

But he stopped me there: "Pretend you are describing all of this to your son Jesse over the phone. But now add trying to describe an onion, its many layers, its pungent odor, the feel of it, firm yet wet, then describe the color from there. Then describe the pillow and the polka dots of an entirely different texture that doesn't match or fit the texture of translucency. Then explain the tiny hardball dots of fabric that are fuzzy to the touch. This could go on and on, trying to describe a pillow to someone who isn't familiar with fabrics or the era when this cloth was popular—and we haven't even touched on a description of the color of the pink dots yet." He made an exaggerated play, gasping for a long, deep breath...

"Whoa!" I said, interrupting his long tangent. Then, "Wow!" as the crux of the lesson hit me. It all made perfect sense.

"There is much difficulty conveying a concept," he went on, "to one who is not familiar. The limited human mind cannot conceive of the entire construct; each piece needs to be explained in a way that can be understood—with something familiar used in the description to bring an awareness of a like-minded position—ideally by the example of a metaphor or story. When the student gets a piece of the concept, they show excitement or nod the head, instead of staring blankly or changing the subject because they just don't understand." He then stopped and gave me the space to analyze his words.

Oh, wow, I get it. This lesson was for me!

I often move entirely too fast in conversation about spirit, offering my explanations and opinions, eager for a connection, an understanding and a like-mindedness. I get so excited to add a new layer that I often steamroll over whatever progress I have made. I forget to lay sufficient groundwork of description and wait for an agreement that we are in simpatico.

This lesson reminded me that I need to wait for the nod of—*I get it, I'm with you*—before bulldozing ahead, dragging my companion beyond their comfort level and giving answers to questions that they are not yet asking or ready for.

More! I thought with my heart full in anticipation of what I might discover.

"May I have some more, please?" I said exuberantly to my teacher. "However long it takes, or how slowly it needs to be introduced to me, I want more! I want to learn more! I want to fully participate in class! Yes!"

~

Lesson 3:
Headspace Teaching

The teacher I want to have, and the teacher I want to be.

One night in a lucid, interactive dream, I found myself in a college hallway with many classroom doors to choose from. I knew I was there to learn something specific, so I looked closely at each door.

A nice-looking man with a salt-and-pepper beard passed by me, opened the door on my right and went inside. The hinge on the door he opened made a hissing sound, with a controlled, slow close. I decided this was the door and I lunged through it in the nick of time.

I found myself in a large classroom, with seats that went up several rows. The bearded man was at the front. He was the professor. The chalkboard held his name and the title of the class. He carried a conceited air and swaggered about, seemingly drunk on his own power. I decided to see what he had to teach, so I climbed up the stairs to a seat.

I noticed that he held a stranglehold over the students who desperately wanted to pass his class, and he reveled in the power of it. As the class began, I soon saw that there would be no true learning here. As he spit his words toward the students, his tone demeaning, they shrank in intimidation. They were less than, and he felt it was his job to constantly remind them of it. He spoke in a downward cast and verbally degraded the students who didn't offer the right answers. They tried to court his favor, but fear wafted in the air like an ocean fog, fear of not passing the class, visibly worn on their faces. This was his power and he was practiced in its use.

I had seen enough and I stood to leave, making my way down the stairs to the doorway. But he was standing near it and I would have to pass him to escape. He watched me intently, and his eyes turned to a beady glass. The students turned their attention to me as well, relieved for a moment of reprise as he coiled to spring on someone else besides them.

I was aware of the silence in the room as I approached the door, and began to excuse myself for disrupting. He was silent in his watchful distaste of my exit. It wasn't until I reached the door that he used the full range and tone of his voice trying to intimidate and belittle me.

But I would have none of it—I would not cower, and turned to him. "I am not one of your students. I came in thinking the class might be interesting, that I could learn something. But I was mistaken. There is nothing for me here."

He was astute in his own power but held nothing over me. He began looking side to side and behind him, reclaiming the students, expecting their loyalty and their backing of him.

I went on. "Your manner of teaching is not working. Your students are not learning from you, as it is impossible to teach anyone who does not share the same *vibrational level*."

He looked perplexed, so I added, "Headspace! You have to join them where *they* are, in their vibration. And you have to *listen*. You cannot teach from a position of holding yourself above your students, as this will result in keeping yourself apart. But if you can be one with them, you can bring them up to a higher level. In working together, you will truly teach, and the students will truly learn. The rare bonding moments, when resonating together, are when learning happens and students truly hold onto the concept you are trying to convey."

With that I exited the classroom. I had indeed learned something, and perhaps the professor had learned something too.

~

Lesson 4:
Is It Finished?
On Being Human

"Is it finished?" said a voice I heard as I woke one morning.

There was a cheery but teasing tone in another voice that answered back "What?"

"I know you heard me" and at that moment, *I recognized that it was something inside of me asking the question. I could hear it, but the words were not coming from my mouth, they were coming from within me. I heard the question asked again:*

"Is it finished?"

"What?" the other voice replied again, as the teasing continued.

"You know what - is it finished?"

Who was talking? I wondered, as I sat up groggily, taking note that I was alone in my room.

During my life I have certainly learned to go by my gut feeling, and my gut was telling me loud and clear that it was *me* asking the questions—it was my own soul. My best *felt* answer is that I was talking to my teacher/guide and what I was asking about, again, would be another guess.

One could say it was about this book you are now reading. At the time it was in the editor's hands after months and months of adding and mixing all of the ingredients it took to create it. It was in a state of percolating, cooking, and growing into what it is meant to be—except that I keep opening the oven door, so to speak, as I continue having vivid and perceptual dreams and I am compelled to write about the lessons and teachings from those dreams and send the new material to the editor with, "Just this one more story, then it's done."

Honestly, that is not what I *felt* the conversation was about. As I lay in the darkness thinking about it, I drifted off to sleep again. Then I received this very powerful precognition dream-experience.

I was sitting on a simple wooden bench with my earthly father who had passed on many years ago. I had loved and trusted him so very much, I recognized him immediately, but in my dream, he seemed every bit a teacher/guide as he did the father I remember.

He was still the handsome dark-haired man I had known and loved, but now he was wearing a bright white-linen caftan. Although we were sitting next to each other on the same bench, he sat facing east, and I was defiantly facing west. We were not in this earthly world, but in a place of timeless peace, and I didn't want to leave it. I was feeling every bit the stubborn daughter/student. Our conversation went like this:

"I don't want to go there," I said. "I'm no good at it. I don't want to do it. Everyone else is better at it than me." And with that statement, I had a visual of many students, their heads down in study or taking tests, young college students who seemed okay with what they were doing, but I didn't want to go and join them.

"You are doing much better than you think you are," he said.

I dragged out a, "Nooo...," like a whiny teenager. "I don't want to go." And in protest I picked up a clear plastic bag full of vile and disgusting human parts, urine, bone, snot, veins, skin and blood, and held up the bag for him to see, and said, "Being human is disgusting. It is heavy and smelly and harrrrrd," I moaned.

He laughed at the sight of this bag full of slimy earth parts.

Ahh, I thought. *That laugh!* I had missed it for so very long, my dad's laugh.

Right in the middle of our serious discussion, I had tickled him, even in my defiance, and now both of us were laughing as we looked at the gory bag full of the physical of being human.

We were still laughing, but I knew the seriousness of our conversation was coming round again.

"I know you can do it," he said, "and I will help you. What if I was to promise to stay with you, and get you through it? What if I personally guarantee that you will graduate this time?"

I knew I had lost the argument, and that I would end up coming back here again, I trusted his words and knew he would stand by me, but still held onto a childish defiance, and would savor the last word in my defeat. I added a stubborn moan or two as we stood together, and he just smiled at me, knowing that he had won.

The next thing I remember is the dark—a comforting blackness that was rich and thick and completely pure. This velvety void was everything and nothing at the same time. It was all around me, but I wasn't afraid. I felt loved and held in a contented state of nothingness.

I saw a light, opposite of me in the dark, as if a light at the end of a tunnel, and as I came closer to it and looked inside, I could see my life as it was being played out, this life, the one I am living right now.

I could see the part my father had played in my life for the mere sixteen years we had together before he died and left me. But now I was seeing with spiritual eyes and I knew with all certainty that he had never left me, especially after his physical death. I could see that he was still so very much with me, and always had been.

There had been a plan; his leaving me had purpose. He left me with a loving physical memory of him, a father and his young daughter, and a memory of all we had shared together, and the unreachable ache of things we would never share again. His early death was meant as a catalyst to spark my curiosity—that I might search for him through all manner of personal study and research of supernatural phenomenon. This was to be a driving force for my entire life. I wanted to know where he had gone, and what comes next, after you have gone. The answers to these questions are what I have endeavored to learn, explore and share. It is what I have always yearned for.

I wake up on this earthly plane, beautiful in its own right, and wonderful because it was created especially for us, a place to experience and learn. I have joined the many students here, doing my best, working to become the spiritual teacher that I have yearned to be. To that end, I hope this time I will graduate.

~ ~ ~

~ ~ ~

There will always be rocks in the road ahead
They can be perceived as stumbling blocks or stepping stones
It depends on your perspective

~ ~ ~

4

Perception and Perspective

~ ~ ~

A Dream of Ghostly Perspective

My dream began with me nestled in a comfy chair, safe within my own home. I awoke from a nap, groggy and yawning. I lifted my arms out for a good stretch—but stopped short and sat up quickly, hearing a noise in the house. I tried to shake myself out my fog and listen.

My attention was drawn to the upstairs balcony. There was a woman looking over the balcony and down into the sunroom where I was nestled. She was about fifty years old, with salt-and-pepper hair, and she was looking right at me! How long had she been there? I swear she was looking directly at me. I noticed she had a bit of a smile on her lips, and she seemed totally comfortable in *my* home!

After looking at me for a moment or two, she slowly turned away and out of my sight. My mind began to race. "Oh, no! I have a ghost in my house! There is a ghost in my house!"

I tried to get a grip over myself, easing out from under the blanket, and slowly rose from the chair—but my eyes never left the balcony where she had stood.

I tried to talk myself out of being scared, telling myself she hadn't seemed mean or scary in any way, she even had a kind of smile on her face when she looked at me. I decided to show her kindness and compassion, because I thought she might be confused too, maybe scared. Perhaps I could tell her to look for the light and assist her to the Other Side where she belonged.

Though my eyes still seemed a bit blurry from sleep, I noticed some things that seemed out of place. The room looked different.

Carefully, quietly, I began looking about my home. It all looked so different. A large yellow sectional was next to my chair, surrounded by new tables and lamps, and it all had more of an upscale style than my own furniture. I noticed the color changes. The walls were painted different colors—bright and bold yellows, oranges and reds, colors I would have loved to eventually try—but before I went to sleep, the walls were white.

This was really confusing. This *was* my home, the same 1970s Frank Lloyd Wright contemporary style, complete with a second-floor balcony. While I admired the decor, I was trying to remember, when or how had it all changed? Was I still asleep, somehow? Perhaps caught in some kind of dream state?

Then a realization came over me. The location was the same—but everything else was different.

I took a few steps toward the stairway, climbing slowly, and found a spot to peek at the woman safely between the wooden railing slats. She paid no attention to me and continued about her business of setting up lights and Christmas decorations. It seemed she wasn't interested in me at all, almost as if she couldn't see or hear me.

I was shocked at my trepidation, but boldly took a few steps. This was *my* house! I would not be ignored. I was not invisible! Then it hit me—*Wait, was I invisible?* Was the reason my house was different, that someone else seemed to be living here, because *I* was dead? *Was I the ghost?*

"No, that's impossible," I told myself. "I would know if I had died. And I would see my relatives or God or at least a tunnel of light…"

Then I worried, why had I not crossed over? Was I stuck in a never-ending nightmare of missing the boat and not going to Heaven?

I was in my house, but I was lost. With this realization, somewhere from deep within me came a wailing of fear, pain, and woe. This guttural uttering was scary, yet the woman seemed not to hear it.

But the dog at her feet surely did, and he snapped to attention, his head suddenly appearing between the slats of the stairs and snarling at me. I was immediately terrified of him. *He* could see me. I took a step back in fear of his snapping, and thought, "*I'm still afraid of dogs.*" It's a fear I've carried since childhood. Now, even dead, I was still scared of dogs. "So, I guess I'm still me," I said to myself.

On the steps above me was a canister vacuum cleaner. I raced to position myself behind it, something physical between me and the dog. Attached at the vacuum's side was a long hose, and I waved it wildly at the dog in a show of force, the hose my protector, as the dog lunged and barked at me.

Then, my fear seemed to spark the vacuum to start, and the loud engine noise sent me back a few steps. The dog also backed up, bewildered.

I was trapped there on the stairs, waving this hose about. Then the dog regrouped and began to lunge at me again, and my fear started up the vacuum again. And as this comedy played out for the second time, the woman ran down the stairs to shut off the vacuum and yelled at the dog to be quiet.

Then I watched her stop and take a moment to assess the situation, and I saw it. A look came over her face, a recall of events, that shape she had seen that had seemed to move out from under the blanket. Had she seen a face in the chair? What about the dog's strange behavior and that weird crying sound she had heard? And now the vacuum seemed to have a mind of its own, turning on and off with nobody here. She looked about her. Was somebody here?

I am a ghost! I thought. For whatever reason, I had slept through my own death and I was stuck here between a dog and a vacuum cleaner.

Scared and confused, I began to feel angry at the fact that I had been left out of the loop of eternal placement. I'd been left here in my last comfortable spot, eternity in a cushy chair. Perhaps this was where I had died?

I now had a lot to ponder and, apparently, I would have a lot of time to do just that.

I awoke, for real this time, wondering if indeed I had ever spent time after a life as a ghost, because all of my feelings of confusion and fear seemed so real.

I sat here and wondered about the salt-and-pepper haired woman and her confusion and fear, because I had felt hers, too. I began to think, then hope, that because of the smile she had seemed to give me, she would feel compassion for my situation and perhaps would come to the same conclusion I had, to be kind and compassionate and try to assist me to the Other Side.

~ ~ ~

Perception Can Be a Fishy Thing

I had a really awesome dream-experience in which I was perfectly content to be underwater. I was in a stream, cool and clear, and I was just hanging out in a calm protected pool surrounded by rocks. I was enjoying the freedom of the water, with almost no movement needed to stay in position, not really floating, just using soft movement to remain buoyant and in place. The clear liquid pulsed through me and around me, above me and beneath me, all of the time.

Deep into this dream, I noted lucidly, "Oh, wow. I'm a fish!" I had no idea what kind of fish, and not really caring, I was just enjoying the beautiful ease of my life in my watery home.

I watched for a nibble, looking from side to side, when I noticed something moving. Though my vision was blurry, I looked up and made out three beings standing over me, well above the waterline. I didn't know what they were, but they were much larger than me.

I was extremely curious about these creatures towering over me. I had never seen anything like them before, and though I was outnumbered and outsized, I was excited and curious. I must have stayed there a bit too long though. I felt myself being lifted from the water—my dream ending just about the time my life as a fish did, too.

I woke up still feeling the cool temperature of the water, in total recall of my blurry water vision and the three images that would end my life then and there. This was a sincerely awesome perspective. *I was a fish! I had remembered a lifetime of being a fish!*

~ ~ ~

"If you judge a fish by its ability to climb a tree,
it will live its whole life believing that it is stupid."

~ Albert Einstein

~ ~ ~

~ ~ ~

Success

One cannot measure a personal mission
by how much was accomplished while here
great or small in the degree of difficulty
the Human experience is invaluable and precious
and to be celebrated as successful
by the unseen ripples of effectiveness

~ ~ ~

5

Of Deep Thinkers

We are all individual examples of God
And we share the same consciousness

~ ~ ~

The Wind Has a Face, and I Have Seen It

The summer of 2014, my husband Chris and I were doing a lot of camping and enjoying nature at it's finest. We slept in a nice clean trailer at night. The daylight hours were filled with hiking and riding ATVs. Afternoons, we usually spent enjoying the warm sunshine in my favorite birthday present—a cozy hammock set up for reading and taking afternoon naps.

One particular morning, I had tuckered myself out during a long morning hike and returned to camp for a restful lunch before our afternoon activities.

The day was becoming windy and anyone who knows me at all has heard me say, "I hate the wind!" But, for now, it was still warm and sunny, with the possibility of a storm blowing in later that evening, so I wanted to take advantage of the rest of the day outside. I crawled into the hammock with a book and a fuzzy blanket, so that only my face and hands were exposed to that dreadful element.

The sun was warm between sandy gusts of air, and the breeze was just enough to keep a gentle sway to my cradle where I lay snuggled and safe. Warm face, full tummy, and the gentle swaying gave way to small nap'ettes between reading paragraphs. I was so relaxed that I decided to just give in and take a full-on nap. I put my book down and pulled the blanket all the way up to my neck, then began to brace myself as another gust built strength.

Then I saw her. *Yes, Her...* the wind is feminine!

She was running toward me, tall and slender, dressed in a long soft, rose-colored dress of sparkling silk, the sunlight reflecting rays of golden thread. It was beautifully tailored, and belted to fit her slender curves. Her soft brown hair was long and curled, partially hidden under a loose hood that framed her face.

She was running with her flock—the gusts of wind—her "children" of all sizes, big and small. They were grey in color, and looked a lot like the tops of an ice-cream cone, with a twist on top. She gathered them all around her as she ran, coming closer and closer to me. The gusts were all around and in front of her, her arms reaching outward, leading and guiding them to gather and stay close to her, they her flock and she their mother.

I noticed only her gown and hair moving as she swept along. She was not windblown, messy or tangled—not a hair out of place. She was coming up on me now, and I could clearly see her face. Beautiful, with the softest doe-brown eyes, and though she wore no smile, she wasn't sad either—she was just busy tending her flock.

As she came even closer I thought we would make eye contact, as I was gazing directly at her and quietly holding my breath. She made no note of me though, but merely continued to run while looking after her children—until I felt a powerful swoosh as she ran directly through me. I braced myself against the strong rush of her passing, and she was gone.

I sat still for the longest time, mystified by what I had just witnessed and felt. "What the?" was all I could utter. I said it aloud two or three more times before laughing out loud as I exclaimed, "I saw her! I really saw her!" I decided that I would never think negatively about the wind again, because I know now that the wind is a living element. *She has face, and she is beautiful!*

~~~

The Yin and Yang of a Complete Soul

In Chinese philosophy, yin and yang (also yin-yang or yin yang, yīnyáng "dark-bright", "negative-positive") describe how seemingly opposite or contrary forces may actually be complementary, interconnected, and interdependent in the natural world, and how they may give rise to each other as they interrelate to one another.

—Source: Wikipedia

The following came to me beautifully wrapped within a dream. It was given to offer clarity that, *yes—we are more than just our body.*

The conceptual leap of this story is that the soul within our body is but a mere fragment of the entirety of our soul. Bear with me here and I will do my best to convey the beautiful message I received.

In the dream, I was walking down the sidewalk of a big city, passing shops with big-mirrored windows. I caught a reflection of myself in the window of a particular shop, and stopped short. As I stood there looking, I thought—*something is missing*—and I felt a deep longing surge from within me.

It became a strong desire to show a more authentic version of myself. I went inside the store and I couldn't control the force that drove me into a drastic cutting of my long hair into a very short, spiky cut. I had never worn my hair this way before, and I looked so very different from the me I had always known. As I stood in front of that mirror, examining this part of me, I knew I wasn't finished.

My next stop was into a clothing shop, where I tried on different outfits. The likeness of the story of the Three Bears was not lost on me, as I tried on the first outfit and it felt too fancy and frilly. The second outfit was too bold—dark leather and jeans—it had a hardness that felt too masculine. The third outfit seemed to reflect a piece of each of the first, some denim but with a soft fabric in the center over the chest, like a flowing shield of femininity against the stiff denim. This one felt just right, both feminine and masculine at the same time. Though I looked very different, I still felt very much like *me*.

I left the shop and walked back out to the street, still feeling an inexplicable loneliness.

I had only taken a few steps down the sunlit walkway when I saw a man standing at the crossway of two streets. I stopped in my tracks and thought—*Oh my God, he is BEAUTIFUL.*

I cannot insert the masculine word "handsome" here, for he was beautiful beyond my ability to describe. The shape of his nose and chin, his face a lustrous quality, his eyes loving and soft, his lips parting in an inviting smile, his blond hair fell to his shoulders, and he dressed in a white-cotton draped robe. The sun held nothing over him; he radiated his own light, his skin luminescent. He exuded a distinct masculine energy, and I was immediately drawn to him, unaware of moving my feet.

I approached as if I knew him, without any thought of rejection. His smile grew as he saw me, his hands opening. As I reached him, he picked me up and held me in his arms. I melded into him, as close as I could get, my arms around him, my face buried into the nape of his neck—and we both delighted in the reunion with our "other half."

This was a completely physical encounter, a physical expression of love, but not in a sexual sense; this was a physical completion of the "other" part of me. It was a reunion of a soul existing in separate parts, yin and yang, a feminine energy exploring the masculine contained within her, and the masculine expressing a found feminine softness. We were each discovering our opposites—one living as male, one as female—joining together again, the soul complete. When a soul is complete it is neither gender, it is the whole of their unity, a perfectly balanced loving energy.

The embrace was coming to an end, and my complete understanding of the connection would fade. We were to be separated again, leaving behind a glimpse of something previously unknown; something longed for in the body here on earth that can't simply be created, replicated or even easily explained.

We both felt a desperate attempt for one lasting touch through our tears of goodbyes, each trying to hold onto the memory of the sweetness of being whole again.

I cried out, "I do not even know what to call you when I need you."

And an answer came, not in words, but as a name on a piece of paper, it read: *Angel.*

"I am to call you Angel?"

With that, the dream ended. I lay in the dark, feeling the ache of physical emptiness—though also grateful for the memory of eternal love, a love of myself and love of the one I would call Angel, who is the other part of me, who is also me.

~ ~ ~

Paquise and Karma Speaking

There are mornings that I wake myself up speaking a different language. It is not the English that I understand and speak in my waking hours. It lasts for a few fleeting moments as reality pours in around the words and they cease, and I am left to wonder where they came from. What is left are my questions and a few unfamiliar sentences or words that I try to capture in my journal to look up later, googling websites for some kind of translation and meaning. Once, the language was German, and I was speaking it fluently, and thick with accent as the words rolled off my tongue. On another occasion, I believe it was Polynesian, and it was accompanied by a visual of being male, and I was yelling something sounding like a command as I paddled on a wooden boat near a plush green island. I was in full voice and wore no shirt in the visual, and saw deep brown skin over a thick arm, and it was mine. As in so many of my other experiences, this was not a dream—I was completely awake.

This morning, I was repeating a sentence in Spanish, or French? And since I don't speak either language, this definitely left an impression. I wanted to remember the words, so I wrote them down in the dream journal that I keep on the bedside table. I awoke saying out loud, "PAQUISE les peoples."

I sat up, fully awake, thinking, *What does this mean?"*

I went to my computer to look it up and found this article in a Google search. Ahh, I thought, very interesting stuff. And in the definition, Paquise and Karma came up: "These individuals are born to have faith in their own process of evolution, also opening up to others safely and offering up their own views—a life purpose is usually not something easily accomplished."

Whooh! I couldn't make this stuff up! It went on to say, "You will encounter obstacles in the field of faith and openness. The deepest aspirations for you and the very purpose of your destiny are to go in the direction of an inner journey rather than an external one.

"A career is never an integral part of a broader and deeper quest," the article continued. "The most important work is always done on the 'inside.' You need a lot of space and time for yourself, moving towards independence, while spending much time alone, rarely sharing your inner thoughts because of fear to be ridiculous. Unfamiliar with your own limitations, it can happen that sharing everything you have leads to a feeling of betrayal, being wronged or misunderstood.

"Almost all with these vibrations," the author continued, "have incisive minds, the kind of spirit who can read between the lines. With all that is necessary to become thinkers, writers, mystics or internationally known scholars, many pursue advanced studies and research in philosophy, mathematics, physics, religion, metaphysics or psychology. They want to know how the human being works, how life works, searching for a deeper wisdom that eludes ordinary looks."

Wow, all of this from three unfamiliar words, and yet it is a mouthful of spiritual teaching, and the Universe at work.

~ ~ ~

Somebody is Going to Heaven Right Now

I just have to share the sweet wisdom of my six year-old grandson Jude.

We were playing in a swimming pool together, squeezing in the last few hours of summer, when dark clouds began to roll in around us and it was going to rain.

Jude called out to me, "Grandma, look!" His head was tilted upward and he was pointing to a small patch of blue sky still untouched by the darker clouds, rays of sunlight were streaming through, creating ribbons of beautiful light. "See that, Grandma. That means somebody is going to Heaven, right now."

I marveled at how aware this little boy is and how deeply he thinks about all manner of things, and agreed that yes, what a grand entry to Heaven the streaming sunlight would be, a beautifully illuminated staircase showing us the way home. I could not resist scooping him into my arms—I just had to hug this little man as I thanked God for him, and for all of the deep thinkers in the world, young and old.

~ ~ ~

Pieces of the Whole

As I was working on this book, I asked for inspiration from the dreams I have recorded in my journals, and this teaching dream popped up—so I am compelled to include it. It's short, but it gave me a lot of clarity about who we all really are and exactly how we came about.

In the dream, I was sitting on the floor with a little girl, whom I recognized immediately, though I don't have an opportunity to see her very often. Vanessa doesn't talk much around me because she is shy, and so I do not feel that I know her as well as I would like to.

I was shown that, in the dream, she was there as a representation, and that she was in my dream to play the part of humanity.

On the floor between us was a beautifully embroidered clutch bag, embellished with sparkling jewels and sewn with golden thread. She and I had found common ground here, both admiring the bag's perfection and beauty. We could see that the beautiful bag was alive and held its own consciousness.

Then, before our eyes the bag changed from what was once whole and alone unto itself; now it separated into many pieces. Each piece was individual and very much alive, each holding its own identity and consciousness. None of the pieces were exactly alike in shape or size; some still carried an attached jewel, some were a jagged piece of silky fabric, and others still held some of the golden thread. Though each piece still held a resemblance to the whole bag in some small way, they did not recognize each other as being a part of the whole anymore. Each piece was now an individual with its own ideas and constructs.

I then found myself explaining to humanity that each piece is necessary and together we make up the whole. Before becoming individuals, we were once a piece of a beautiful, unified consciousness.

I knew that it was not my task to try to put the pieces back together, but that I was to assist in the acceptance and understanding that we are all one, all of us a piece of the Source—God—and that it was his decision to separate us into living individual pieces of consciousness. It is for us to recognize that we are more alike than we previously realized.

~ ~ ~

Us, Them, We

The day had barely arrived and only the softest of light had found its way into my room. I was ready for a cup of coffee and the start of a new day when I heard the familiar voice of my spirit schoolteacher saying, *"Ask the question."*

So, I sat back down on the edge of the bed and began recalling the night's dream that was still drifting in the air around me.

Something amazing was happening on the moon. It was an event of huge proportions, possibly changing all our lives, or at least how we saw our place in the Universe.

People were looking up, in deep thought; some dusting off telescopes brought up from basements. Others were simply going about their days, paying no mind to the excitement that was building all around them. They either didn't care or wouldn't let themselves believe. Perhaps this was their way of fending off fear of the event, or appearing foolish—believing in something more than what they could see, taste, or feel. They just pretended there was nothing happening and went about their day saying aloud, "that all of this was much ado about nothing."

I was in the pack of the excited ones who were looking up at the sky—hoping for *something* to see, wanting to be a witness to whatever it was—in real time, with my own eyes.

Some hopped into their cars and headed to the space observatory because they really needed to know, they couldn't wait for the evening news; they had to see it for themselves and as up close as they could be to whatever it was on the moon.

Others were people who felt the need to be present at the event. A woman I actually knew in waking life represented this group, and she was in the process of changing her life after a bitter divorce and custody battle. She had taken the time to heal and nurse her wounded heart, and I had seen Facebook posts filled with pictures of her climbing mountains and hiking near the sea. She's been exploring herself and expanding her life through one adventure after another.

In the dream, she suddenly broke from our group and ran to a large metal cylinder rocket and flew off into the sky toward the moon. (Remember this is a dream, so this would be completely possible, right?) She would soon be there and witness the event first-hand, and perhaps even play a role in it, fulfilling her need to explore all possibilities. She felt no fear or hesitation; she found a way to get herself there, and off she went. This was my dream.

"Ask the question," I heard the teacher say again.

"Okay," I thought, and my mind recalled all the different people I saw in the dream. The event on the moon was the catalyst, but the real story was about the people living below, and the many different ways they responded when faced with something different and unfamiliar. Some reacting in joy, excitement, fear, annoyance, ignorance; others determined to explore, to solve, and to become a part of it.

I asked my teacher, *"Why? Why are there so many different reactions to the same event? Why do people who seem the same, react so very differently from one another?"*

Before I could finish asking these questions, the big question, the one I really wanted to ask, rose and made its way to the forefront of my mind, and I recognized it as one we have all asked from time to time. It is the question that I had accepted that I may never know the answer to in this lifetime, but since my teacher was encouraging me, I took a deep breath and asked,

"What is our purpose?"

And the answer immediately poured into me, as if poised and patiently waiting for me all along. It had always been within my reach, just outside my awareness, the answer now audible, tangible:

We are all God's self, expressed in a physical form,
each of us a personality playing a role of exploration
and awareness of self, who is God.
We are all needed, as each one of us is unique and
there is purpose to that, as each one of us has a role
to be played out in our own individual level of awareness.
Each path back to God is valued for the experience
that will be shared with our maker, who is US.

~ ~ ~

Balcony Belief

In a dream-experience, I was standing on a stone balcony—one among millions on other balconies, thousands of rows of them—all facing the square where God was.

I couldn't see God from my section of the balcony, which had a rounded corner, and a footing was blocking my view, but I enjoyed the energy and the sound of it all. Those around me were happily singing and praising God in worship, and I was excited to be there.

I was made to know that I was experiencing Heaven, and I felt completely honored to be shown this, but this scene seemed to just go on and on and on. After a while, I turned to my companion/guide who had brought me there, my mind full of questions.

"What else goes on in Heaven?"

"This is Heaven," he answered, "and this is what we do here. We worship and praise God as he stands before us, letting us adore him."

I took a step backward. "What?" I said, questioning openly and shaking my head irreverently. I just couldn't swallow this. I was expected to take a giant step backward? Was I to step back into blind faith and a belief system I had left behind many years ago?

"Really? This is it? God just wants us to stay here and worship him, forever? This is what we do after we die?"

My companion seemed confused by my questions and my lack of belief, like how dare I not accept this as truth? He began to lose his patience and I felt his love for me fade. *This confused me*, because in my awakening experiences, my guides had never grown angry at my lack of immediate understanding or acceptance. They had always been patient teachers as they showed me new concepts and information.

No, the loving God I have come to know is not a huge ego needing constant praise and adoration—I just couldn't buy it. As I continued my defiance, the guide began to change and become dark. The singing began to slide off key and was not as beautiful as it had first seemed.

Eventually, the entire scene became warped, and my companion began to shrink like a balloon, as if he had been animated.

I woke up knowing that I had *not* viewed Heaven, but only a human version that many believers hold—making it real in a sense. We must challenge the old, embedded fear-based belief systems and come to know that it is God who loves *us* unconditionally, not the other way around. He created us not to behave as a multitude of worshipers fulfilling his ego; but as living, breathing *reflections of himself* on a journey of experiencing the physical realm and all that is, then returning to share the experience.

Only days after this dream-experience, I attended a reunion with my husband in his childhood home town, a lovely small town full of like-minded members of the same local church, but it still caught me a little off guard, as a simple conversation soon slid into one of religion.

The gentleman leading the conversation was used to missionary work and was quite fervent in his attempt to convert my husband and me to his own way of thinking. I felt an urge to retort with my own newfound teachings, but I did not; because I have learned that these types of debates do not teach, yet harden the other's resolve to hold on to what is familiar.

Instead, I gracefully gave him the floor and found myself in a kind of admiration of the ardor of his faith, his commitment to it, and his willingness to share it. I have thought about him since our meeting, because there was a love of God in his message, and there is no need to find argument in that. At the same time, I find comfort in my own station of peace as I share the messages I receive, hoping they might lead to a reassessment of what we have been taught, and what we truly believe.

The sharing of these experiences is not with the intent of degrading anyone's belief or faith, as I believe *all* are important in our human quest for cultural involvement and acceptance and that *all* roads that bring us closer to a personal relationship with God are important.

I am deeply grateful for the powerful dream-experiences I have been given, they envelope me in a profound peace and joy upon waking from these powerful nighttime communications. My personal feeling is that these dream interactions are shown to me (and I am able to see them and remember them) because I ask and am totally open to receiving new insights about the greater realities and myself. We can all ask for them, and we can all receive.

~ ~ ~

Being human, with all of its strengths and frailties
is the job and the path that we are propelled to
seek out and accomplish
Just be Human
We are here so that God can experience
His own imagination

6

Of Grief and Loss

~ ~ ~

The Smells You Remember

For some people it could be tobacco or pipe smoke, old spice cologne, the scent of fresh cut grass, a lusty red rose, leather and shoe polish, or even the musty odor of closet mothballs. They are the "special smells" that bring a loved one to mind. This morning as I folded the ingredients together to make fresh breakfast muffins, I was enveloped in the fresh smell of peaches.

The wafting scent overtook all of my senses as I peeled, sliced and diced the juicy fruit, as its unmistakable juicy aroma quickly transported me. I was once again a young woman, having just been released from the hospital with my first child, a beautiful baby girl. I was afraid, more than in pain, fearing that I wouldn't know how to stop her crying by myself. The responsibility of her was daunting, and I was filled with self-doubt as I lay in bed at my mother's, my old home, in my old room.

I was recalling it all, my mother bringing in a tray of sandwiches; off to the side of the tray was a fragrant bowl of peaches, preserved from her garden last summer. I cannot explain the comfort and courage my mother's peaches gave me that day as I took my baby in my arms and took over her care.

My mother would later teach me to can and preserve my own peaches, from my own garden. I had four more beautiful babies come into my life, and just like John Denver sang, I fed'em on peaches.

Eventually, I bounced back to reality in my own kitchen at sixty-three years old, recalling my mother who passed away last year. I miss her every day, but especially on this day, as the oven bakes and the air is filled with the sweet aroma of peaches and the sweetest memory of a loving mother who taught me how to mother.

~ ~ ~

You Have Me Laughing Through My Tears

My husband Chris and I decided to steal away for an afternoon movie date. I made a quick run to the market for a few snacks to tuck into my purse.

It was Christmastime, and the smell of cinnamon sticks filled the air as I passed rows of oranges and a man dressed in red, ringing a bell over a bucket. I was almost to my car when I noticed two young sisters walking arm in arm into the store. Then it hit me hard and fast—the grief of her loss—*I miss my sister!*

Kaylyn had been gone for over a year, and her birthday had passed just a few days before. I gave no acknowledgment to a car that was waiting for my spot, and my tears turned into sobs. Then, a deep, guttural sound welled from deep within me, a moan of pain and loss, grief in its rawest form.

As I finally climbed into my car, tears rolling down my face, I heard her. *"Hey, I thought we already went through all of this!"*

"Kay?" I whispered, not yet starting my car. Then I started on a roll without a breath between. "I miss you. I miss our childhood Christmas's. We should have been closer!" It all spilled out.

She calmly replied, *"We are close now, aren't we?"*

"Yes, I know, we are," I said out loud, and thought, Kaylyn has been very generous to me with her visits from the Other Side, and so I added, "I guess I'm just being human."

She laughed. *"Well, yes, you are still human, so I guess it's alright. But really, don't cry, I'm fine."*

"Kay, your pain, is it gone?" I asked, still parked in my spot. "And you have more energy now?"

"I feel fucking FANTASTIC!"

"Kay!" I said, stunned. "I've never heard you talk this way before."

"I know. I'm doing a lot of things now I haven't done before, or at least not for a very long time."

My crying subsided and, in a kind of shock, I began to laugh. Kaylyn was swearing? I had *never* even heard her swear before—and this one, the big daddy of swear words—Whoa! It sounded so foreign coming from her, I found it hilarious! My laughter grew into almost snorting, with a runny nose and tears streaming down my cheeks.

I'm losing it, I thought to myself, catching a glimpse of myself in the rearview mirror.

After a few moments, I calmed myself. "Kay, thank you for always showing up. I know we are closer now than ever before." I could almost feel her smile.

"I'm here, and we are both OK," she said. *"Oh, and about the swearing part, let's just keep that between us, okay?"*

This got me laughing again. She was still worried about getting into trouble with Mom.

"Love you, Kay," I whispered to her as I let the connection fade.

I took stock of myself, now, blotchy red cheeks, mascara circles under my eyes. I looked a sight. Yet, I smiled at the emotional rollercoaster I have been riding, from sobs to laughter, in less than five minutes, another world record.

"Thank you, my Sister. Thank you for the comfort you bring, we are and will always remain sisters, and you have me laughing through my tears."

~ ~ ~

To a Young Widow

This spring the world lost one of the good ones, a wonderful, loving caring soul, his name was Brady Shepherd, and he was my nephew.

I have long admired his commitment to a cause after recognizing a need for families left in grief after losing a loved one to suicide. He knew by experience that the condolences after this kind of death are not as forthcoming as they should be.

Grieving loved ones are left with unanswered questions and a need to share the story of who their loved one really was in life, and not just the end that was chosen. One can never conceive of the catalyst that will change the course of one's life, but the suicide of his sister Marci was Brady's.

He started a foundation and website, *No Story Left Untold*, to share their story and talk with others left behind in the grief and loss from suicide. Brady created a safe, non-judgmental zone where healing and understanding is offered.

The loss of Brady will be long felt by those of us who knew him and by so many that did not. A momentary blink of an eye on a dark highway in the early morning hours took Brady from this world, his work far from over, and the why of taking one so committed to doing such good work is not easily understood.

What I share here Brady gave to me a few days after his death. I had asked him to come, and I wrote as he gave me the words he would like his sweet young wife Danielle to be left with. His words came to me in poem:

Dear Danielle,

Though our days together here
have now come to a close
as I have lifted to a place unknown
and left you there alone

I will make a place for us
for when your day will come
hold tightly to our memories
and know that we were one

Think of words so sweet and days so bright
and all the smiles we gave
The love we shared still lingers here,
beyond a mortal grave.

We made the most of what we had
and gave it back to one another.
We were enough and now live on
in glory of each other.

Now I must go and you must stay
to finish what we started.
But someday soon we'll be entwined
as if we never parted.
Stay strong, my love,
for I am near and smiling back at you.
Complete your days in happiness.
This I ask of you.

Move forward in your life, my love.
Let others help you through.
And in the evenings, dream of me
and all the things we'll do.

Together we will be again,
to hold each other tight.
Until we meet again someday,
I'll hold you in my light.

With all my love, Brady

~ ~ ~

Yes, you can save the world.

The Power of Thought can change
the very structure upon which you live,
the only limitation is what is
placed on you by yourself.

You must not rely on an
intervention from an outside source,
but rather to find the healing source,
you must look within.

~ ~ ~

7

Making Change

~ ~ ~

Dreams of a Moneyless Future

Last night, I had what I will to refer to as a wise dream. I was given knowledge along with a visual, and the impact of this message imprinted on me because my Angel Sister delivered it. I didn't see her face but I knew it was she, and I used her name several times within the conversation.

I noticed her hands though, as they were in front of a pile of grayish-brown ovals, with black marks on them. She picked one up and held it out so I could clearly see that it looked like a rock, and the black markings that were etched into it, looked like an upside down letter 'A', I watched as she purposely dropped it. I could tell by the way it fell and barely bounced that it was not a rock, and that it was extremely lightweight.

My thought was that it was wooden, and I asked her, "What is this, Kaylyn?" She said it was to be the new currency. "Money?" I thought aloud, and she said, "not really money as we have known it, as there will not be a need or a use for dollars. This will be a form of exchange that will be used." I do not remember if she used the word "soon," but I hope so!

In our conversation, she spoke of what was to come, a total breakdown of world currency and basically all worldly stuff. She said that all written laws—political, biblical, and constitutional—would be put aside. For this, I received a visual of them all being tossed aside like outdated textbooks, no longer working within the current curriculum. She said that things would be "starting over," and repeated this for emphasis—a "big start over" or "mulligan coming," so to speak, and we would no longer be held in the dark.

Lastly, she added, "Any laws, if needed, will be scripted in full spiritual light and knowledge of God."

I don't recall the end of our conversation or our goodbyes, but the feeling of her visit and the messages she brought have stayed with me.

Whooh! I think a great time is ahead of us, and I hope it comes soon!

~ ~ ~

Pretty Perfect People

Carry your own ego in a small satchel

Last night, I received a dream labeled "Metaphor of world change." Though it was presented in black-and-white, it was very real. All dream indicators (felt senses, even in sleep) pointed to "pay attention" to this one.

The scene was of a grouping of the "Beautiful People," the perfectly sculpted, lean and well muscled, oiled and tan, worthy of magazine covers. I was shown closets filled with stylish clothing and shoes, cases of jewels, expensive cars and homes, all things many of us aspire to have. This gathering of the Beautiful People was an opportunity for them to be seen in all of their glory, each one vying for the attention of the others. *Oh, to be me* was thought, as they caught their own glamorized reflections of perfection.

As I continued to watch this group parade and promenade, I was then given an "under the surface" view of these people. They were so empty, less than hollow, and there was no love to share, only an unrequited love of themselves. There was nothing left to give anyone else. They looked upon life and humanity as steps to their own self-importance, others to serve and adore them in their worldly perfection.

Next, I was shown a world beginning to change and a shift in consciousness was beginning to take hold. A loving, caring, and sharing community was emerging; seeing beauty in selfless service to one another. A beautiful tapestry of everyone being needed and interconnected was being created, and this tapestry of woven love and caring was now the earth's perfection.

Unable to grasp the changing world around them, the Beautiful People grew visibly concerned. Would there be no one left to worship them? They could not wrap their heads around this change—that all must love and help one another—and those who cannot or will not change, as the world evolves without them, will not be allowed to stay, as they will taint this new perfection.

The next scene was a huge white porcelain bowl; and the Beautiful People were lying in it, unable to climb out. The entirety of it was filled, stacked side by side with them, and their fear was palpable.

My heart broke for them as I watched this play out, a change was needed from within each one of them; a softened and tolerant heart, a gratitude for all that had been given them, and a giving nature. No one could do this for them, and it could not be purchased or borrowed.

I pleaded with them, but they would not or could not hear me. I was powerless to help them. They began to slide downward in the slippery bowl toward the black hole at the bottom, fighting furiously and blaming each other, pushing and climbing over one another to distance themselves from the dark hole, and those pushed to the bottom were unable to stop themselves from sliding in. It was a horrible thing to watch, even worse to feel their fear and my complete inability to help.

I began to notice that after many had slipped down the drain, it was as if it became plugged and some were spewed back out. They were disheveled and dirtied, but now had a new chance to be at the top of the bowl again. Their hateful words of blame continued, though, screaming accusations at one another—all their problems being caused by someone else—and their second chance was ignored.

This awful pattern repeated itself over and over. Each time that five or six went down the drain, three were spat back out, covered in dirty, dark and stinking mire. None looked up, none changed, and none offered a hand to help another. They only pushed, shoved and blamed—all hating the other—blaming the person next to them for their woes.

Selfishness and oneness cannot live in the new world. These people were burdened by their own weight, a love of themselves and all their belongings. The world was changing and growing into a new dimension, and they would not be a part of this great shift. They would need to be stripped of their heavy three-dimensional bodies and old ways of thinking, and this came be in the form of the destruction they now faced.

I was then told they were not going to Hell. Rather, they would be cared for and taught on the Other Side, then eventually reborn into a new fifth dimensional earth of love and compassion. The dream made it clear that not all would survive this coming shift, and all could not stay here for its completion. If one's actions and heart were a hindrance to this change, they would be left behind.

In the end, we are all in charge of our own actions; as the world evolves, there will be no tolerance of blaming another for our downfall, or taking credit for our success.

Let your own actions speak for you in Love and Service to one another—there is no need for fear—find and then reflect the light. The positive frequency of the light will change the world, and all of those in the light will shift with it.

~ ~ ~

Live Each Day to the Fullest, this Gift of Precious Life

Last year I spent several days in the Uinta Mountains, a beautiful Utah range full of trees and grassy meadows—perfect for ATV riding.

I love to be in nature's splendor, taking mental pictures as I ride. It's exhilarating and freeing to ride over dirt and boulders, yet I feel safe underneath my protective, padded clothing and gear. The helmet I wear is a tight fit and it squishes my chubby cheeks, but I'm grateful for the feeling it creates as it seals me inside, setting my mind free to wander as the roar of the engine creates a rhythmic vibrational lull.

The combination of all these conditions creates a perfect opportunity to connect to the Other Side, and I have made a point of using this time to make contact with both my sister Kay and my Mother who recently passed.

This late September morning seemed to come too early, as my husband Chris and I snuggled in our cabin near a warm fire. The season's first snow had fallen the night before and this made me a bit nervous, as I have always been a fair-weather rider. We had purposely planned this trip late in the season in the hope of being full witness to the colorful show of fall with the seasonal changing of leaves to brilliant hues of orange and red.

Uh-oh, I thought, as we prepared to venture out into the wintery weather, because I'm not fan of being cold and winter sports are not my thing.

I had to mentally put on my big girl pants today, along with a few more layers of clothing than usual, to enjoy this ride.

The sky was heavy with fat moisture-filled clouds that hung so low and close to the trails you could stretch out your hand and almost touch them. It created a small visual frame to fit us into, like a pocket of echoes between the white-covered ground and the light-grey sky hanging directly over our heads.

We sat on padded seats, atop a warm and roaring engine, our ATVs following trails through fire-colored trees. There was such splendor in the leaves, each one brilliantly accentuated against the freshly fallen pure white snow. There was a sacred silence in the air and as I marveled at the stunning vistas, I was thrilled to be a part of something very few people experience. I could not contain my joy here in the somber stillness, and squealed with delight as we tore through snow-covered puddles, tossing mud from the meaty wheels, my laughter echoed in every direction.

Frosty ice crystals floated in the air and I excitedly breathed them in. I felt them on my face, but I never noticed the cold. I was having some of the best fun of my life, right here, right now.

I thought of my mother, who had never experienced anything like this. I called out, "Mom! Come, please. Come feel this with me. You have to feel this! Kay, are you there? Please come. I want to share this with you!"

I called out to them several times. The conditions were perfect for our *chats* and this had worked on previous rides. So I had no doubt that I could make contact.

"Come ride along with me today. I want to share this with you!"

It was a few minutes later that I heard my mother, in an audible voice that came into my mind, not my voice, not my thoughts, say something different that was not me.

I heard her say, *"You're not riding horses!"* a personal funny comment my mother and I share. It stemmed from a voicemail message she had left years before when I didn't answer her call, saying, "Where are you? Hiking or out riding horses?"

Now she added, *"Well, this is not something I would expect you to like doing, out here in the cold!"*

Her words made me laugh, because she was exactly right. No one who really knew me would expect to find me out here in the cold. And I laughed because I could *hear* her, and the joy of this, along with the beauty of this day made everything perfect.

I called out to my sister again. "Kay, come ride along with me today. I want to share this beauty with you both. "

I was excited to hear from her, too. *"Okay, let's go!"* she said.

I drew in a deep appreciative breath of the cold frosty air into my lungs and watched the warm steamy wisps escape upon exhaling. I did it again, exaggerating a deep steamy exchange within my lungs, from frosty cold to steamy warmth, appreciating another miracle of the day.

"Can you *feel* this?" I said, and not waiting for an answer, put the motor in gear and flew down the trail, calling out "Stay with me awhile!" I wanted to share the freedom and exhilaration I was enjoying and also the beauty of the world that surrounded me.

When I came upon the largest and deepest puddle of the day, I called out to my invited passengers to "HANG ON!" as I splashed through it as fast as I could go, gunning the gas, and squealing with laughter as the water sprayed a huge wall of water on both sides of the ATV, while I stayed perfectly dry in its wake.

I was smiling ear to ear as I slowed the engine to wipe some collected mud off my goggles and openly addressed my Mother and Sister, but this time in a softer, and more serious tone. "I know that someday you both will have so much to share with me about where you are, and what it is like there; but today, I just wanted to share all of this with you and I really hope you can feel it through me."

The ride continued for several hours, until eventually I lost the feeling of their closeness. It was wonderful to have felt them, like one on each shoulder, on a perfect day of an awesome experience. I don't know if they could feel it, but I do know they appreciated my attempt to share my glorious day, because they left me with a phrase that continually ran through my head the rest of the day and all of the days that have followed:

"Live each day to the fullest, this gift of precious life!"

I promise with all sincerity to make each day count.

The days that follow might not always be as spectacular as this one, but I will make sure to appreciate and use them up, each and every day that is left to me, to the best of its potential. *I promise.*

~ ~ ~

I have always found this bumper sticker interesting. The first time I noticed it, many years ago, I stared at it for a full minute to figure it out. *Cool,* I thought." *Good idea, COEXIST.*

Today, I found myself following this sticker in traffic. It was prominently placed on the back window for all to see. Now stopped at a traffic light, I could really get a good look at the many symbols used to create the word COEXIST.

The traffic light was long and my attention was soon diverted to a car at my right, just two car lengths ahead. The car had its blinker on—left, left, left—hard to miss, and the young woman driving it was looking pleadingly at the driver of the COEXIST car, who was in the lane she wanted to move into—left, left, left.

It seemed a very clear question was being posed here, and the answer also seemed clear, because it was a simple request and an easily accomplished favor. I mean, you could easily help a sister out, do a solid—you know, COEXIST—but the light turned green and all of the cars lunged forward, including the car with the Universal Thought Sticker. I am sorry to report here that Sister Universe continued to move on too, leaving the frustrated driver in the right lane, her eyes pleading for some nice person to make a difference in her day.

No problem. I waved her ahead, and it wasn't a problem. It didn't cost me a thing and no laws were broken. The only thing used was an extra second in my day. Yes, it put me one more car length behind in my lane, on an already busy road to somewhere not that urgent.

I pray that I never run out of these seconds to spare, or ever feel like I don't have enough, hoarding the ones I have instead of thoughtfully spending them to help another and COEXIST.

In conclusion, I make reference to Miss Put It Out There Then Fail To Do It—COEXIST I mean. Of course, you are probably a wonderful person, but perhaps the next time you wash your car or put something into the trunk you might take a brief pause in your busy day to read the words you have put out into the world, because your words say one thing but your actions speak volumes.

Perhaps all of us can take a lesson here, and consider what exactly does COEXIST mean?

~ ~ ~

Calling All COGS

Spiritual teachings can come in the funniest of ways. My daughter Sarah and son-in-law Miah were visiting during Christmas. We decided to have a relaxing night of popcorn and a movie. The movie that was decided by majority vote was called *Idiocracy*. It was about the future of the world getting dumber and dumber, and the thought occurred me that it doesn't matter if you are the only "smart" one in the crowd if all around you are stupid.

The condition of the world in the movie had adjusted downward to the level of the masses. The *spiritual synchronicity* of this scenario was not wasted on me. Only a few days before I had wakened with this sentence in my mind: *"All must be raised together. If one learns—all must be taught, all must be raised—no one is to be left behind."*

The night we watched the movie, after a few hours of sleep I woke up, remembering that I had been dreaming of being in Spirit School. I get so excited when I remember the lessons taught in a dream experience, and this memory was kind of thrown at me as I snapped awake. "Quantum physics"? This not my usual train of thought, umm, ever. So, I thought, *Oh, I've been to Spirit School.* I share here what I was allowed to bring back with me:

Imagine a thick wire coil—clean, shining and totally symmetric—pulled apart and stretched out evenly. Individual cogs or disks float on the inside of each loop of the expanded coil. The coil is so large that there are many individual cogs revealed within the length of the coil—all vibrating, humming and running smoothly within each loop of the coil. They are all level and at exactly the same vibrational frequency, running independently, yet part of the whole. All are needed to run smoothly, all needing to be on the same frequency in order to be geared and moving together, smooth operational gears running in sync with one another, thus propelling and moving the whole. It is a perfect mathematical machine, and *It is Us.*

I was then shown a diagram representing us as a whole, showing me how we are quantum physics and we are all needed in order to run perfectly: not as a Borg Society, but as independently vibrating individuals who are part of the whole. In order to work and move forward, all must raise and vibrate together as one.

This insight was awesome. I awoke thinking, *"I want to learn math!*

Ha, ha, a huge statement for someone who never got math before, or ever really cared that I didn't get it. But quantum physics is all about the math, and fitting together as one, to make perfect the operating machinery of life.

I lay there wishing I had experienced a teacher in life like the one I have in Spirit School. Last night, he looked directly into my eyes and said, *"Don't turn off here. You can get this. Now watch."*

I did. I witnessed and experienced a floating, working example—

a spiraled coil revealing each individual beating, vibrating cog—working as a whole as a means to an end, together. All needed, all important. All must rise together, no one to be left behind.

My Spirit Teacher really cared that I understood this, and I share it here because it is important that we all understand. We cannot rise alone, we must rise together, all included in the whole. Our brothers and our neighbors, all a part of the One.

I am so grateful to have a Teacher who is willing to teach me the mysteries of the Universe. And as I learn, so many more doors are opening, but I am shown that we need to take each other's hands in order to walk through them.

~ ~ ~

On a Dime at the Dollar Store

In this time of reflection and resolution for the coming year, I would like to share a life-affirming experience I had on Christmas Eve.

I found myself in a crowded Dollar Store, just thinking I needed a few more things for my grandchildren. The line was long, but like everyone else there, I wanted to make my Christmas purchase of plastic trinkets of joy, so I waited.

I found myself focusing on the people in the line ahead of me, and an older woman caught my eye, a kindred spirit as her arms were also filled with toys and happy trinkets. She dragged an old zippered pull cart behind her and, as I took notice of her, she instinctively turned to me and smiled and we began a simple conversation.

I pointed to the cart. "Great idea!"

She responded, "Yes, this really helps. I don't live far from here and walk over a lot, but I always seem to find more than my hands can carry back home."

"Oh, yeah." I said in agreement, and shuffled and tightened my grip on my own items that were slipping and shifting. "Grandkids, how can we resist?"

That statement sent both of us into giggles, and a shoulder shrug,

"Yes, those precious grandchildren."

And with that collective agreement, we smiled and our attention went to other things.

After I checked out and my goodies were bagged, I started my car and began my drive home but stopped short as I noticed a commotion in the street. Cars on one side weren't moving and there were people in the street talking on cell phones. I noticed a young pregnant woman kneeling over someone, and then I saw the someone: The little old lady from the store!

"Oh, God, no!" I said aloud as I caught my breath. "Oh, no, no, no!"

How could this have happened? She was just buying presents for her grandchildren, healthy enough to walk to her destination, now lying helplessly still in the middle of the road, knocked out of her shoes, her gifts and the pull cart overturned in the street.

Through the blood on her face, I could see her lips move but that was all that was moving. She lay so very still on that cold road, her arms at her sides, and her legs in a strange posture. I knew she was badly hurt and my thoughts went to unrecoverable aging ailments, broken hips, perhaps back or neck, in the least her bent legs would mean no more walking to the Dollar Store again for a long time, if ever.

I began to cry out for her, wanting to make it all better. I surveyed the situation and the pile of cars behind and at the side of me, with nowhere to pull over. I had no real assistance to give, as the young woman who had hit her was at her side and showing complete kindness. The calls were being made to the police and ambulance, and I felt the pushing of the cars wanting to move on behind me. I inched forward; sickened by the thought of leaving her, but knowing my part in this drama was over.

There would be lessons to learn from this tragedy: a distracted young woman who would forever wish she had taken a second look before making that turn. The ripple effect through the families of all involved, the grandchildren who might never know that Grandma's last thoughts were of them, and the care that would now be needed to help her recover, a new financial struggle, and the relinquishing of an enjoyed freedom of a simple walk to the store, she would now have to adjust to new pains and possibly the ability to live on her own. And so I write this story, for myself and for those who may read it, in hopes of sharing the valuable lesson I received that day:

Take nothing for granted in this life,
because it can all change in one irreversible instant.

One never knows, as we wake, what the day will bring, what may be left undone or unspoken. Is there forgiveness that needs to be given or an act of love or kindness that needs to be shown?

Lastly and maybe the most important lesson of all—if we could imagine the ripple effects of our own actions—how a simple conversation with a stranger can touch our lives forever.

~ ~ ~

A Divine Gathering

~ ~ ~

The silent masses gather
Lyrical sounds vast and acoustic enter the sky
Like a prayer heard around the world
Their voices carry into the depths of the night
Radiant and translucent lights glow
across the vortex of a ceremony
Snow gently sways perpendicular to the wind
Displaying a dance of natures wisdom

Your reflection is seen through mirrors of solid ice
As each of your senses open
An overwhelming feeling of love and diversity circle the mind
Floating souls of ancient travelers crowd the sky
like rows in a stadium
Each to contribute the past and future
Songs sway, stories are shared
And the knowledge
That we so dearly lock within ourselves just seems to spill out

A collaboration of the magnanimous
Because each and every one of us are truly remarkable
The more we share with each other
The more beauty is revealed"

~ Aaron Joseph Clayton

~ ~ ~

8

Reincarnation Stories & Life Purpose

We are here so that God can experience his own imagination

~ ~ ~

Trust the Man, Trust the Lesson

The following is a deeply personal example and affirmation of reincarnation. The intensity of what I was shown, from my father, the man I had loved and trusted most in the world, solidified a deep-seated knowing. Never again, would I doubt the validity of lives lived before or after this one.

As a grieving sixteen-year-old girl, I could not understand where the love and enormity of the energy that was my father could just go away, to be lost forever on a tragic day in 1969. I knew in my heart that he lived on, somewhere, and I wanted answers, I wanted more than faith or a belief of this to be true, and I wanted to feel it, beyond doubt. I was determined to know with an unwavering certainty.

My father was not the harps-and-choir type—*so how was he spending his days there? And where was there?* Did he miss me as much as I missed him? Was he lonely or keeping busy doing Heaven stuff, and what was Heaven stuff?

Since my father's death, I have spent many years studying cases of near-death experiences (NDEs) with an insatiable desire, a propelled quest to find him, to really know where he went and what he was doing. My studies were a safe place to put the grief of his loss, consoling myself during so many years of "quiet" from him, in fact over forty years of silence.

I had thought I was open to receiving messages from him and, during my tearful demands, I would ask why I hadn't heard from him, why not a visit or a dream, why had he not found a way to contact me, the daughter who loved and missed him so much.

One would think after so many years I would have given up, but there was no way that I would ever give him up, not for a chance to see/feel/smell/hear him again.

During a well-timed "accidental" encounter with a friend, I was told about Dr. Michael Newton's book on reincarnation. *Journey of Souls* is a richly detailed accounting of over 7,000 documented case studies of people while relaxed under hypnosis and therapy to control smoking or other additions—and Dr Newton's surprise, when the patients began describing detailed experiences of lives lived before and even in-between lives.

These accounts jelled immediately for me, so many questions were answered and aha moments began to add up. Sometimes I just had to close the book and sit with it all, letting the lesson or example of a particular case waft through me, allowing it pause to collect, and then permeate within me.

The book seemed to open the top of my head with a quickening of knowledge of the Afterlife. My physic abilities began to expand, and my dreams became deeper and richer, more concise in detail. I began to receive messages in my dreams and found it helpful to keep track of these messages. I began keeping a dream journal, practicing and working to become lucid in my dreams, recording the stories received in the dream state.

Then I received the gift of a dream-experience from my beloved father, and the enormity and weight of its message took me some time to process.

It started with me holding a crisp white envelope. The note inside was printed on thick smooth card stock. It was an "Invitation to Meet" with my father, who had passed over forty years ago.

I stood there in the dream, hardly believing my eyes, reading the card over and over, then saying the words aloud, feeling the detail of each word as they left my lips. A joy bubbled from deep within me and could not be contained. To say I was elated would be an understatement.

In my hands, I held detailed instructions of where and when to meet him. It was all laid out within the note, everything I had wanted, I would see him again! All of it was right here in my hands.

Then it hit me, the meeting place was several states away—in the dream—and there wasn't a lot of time to get there.

I quickly threw a few things together and began my journey. I hardly stopped for anything but gas as I drove across cities and states toward my destination. Each time I stood outside my car to fill up the tank, I shared my wonderful news with anyone who would listen. "I'm going to 'meet' with my Dad! I haven't seen him in over forty years. Look, he sent me a note!" The strangers all seemed to share in my excitement, sending me off with the best of wishes for my reunion.

After a few days of travel, I neared my destination. The address on the card was taking me just outside a small Midwestern town. I traveled down a dirt road and watched the house numbers get closer, until they finally matched the numbers on my invitation. I stopped at the mailbox outside an old, modest farmhouse with acres of land between it and the closest neighbor.

I turned off my car and sat there for a moment. My dad was here? I thought about my expectations, or had my excitement left any room for any expectations at all?

It was only at this very moment, as I looked up a hill toward an unfamiliar house in an unfamiliar town, that I wondered, why had he picked such an odd place to meet?

My eyes followed the gravel driveway toward the house, and I noticed a lot of activity at the end of the driveway. I checked my watch. It was only minutes until my appointed time. I took a last look in the rearview mirror, fluffed my hair and touched up my lipstick. He hadn't seen me since I was sixteen. As I got out of the car, I hoped he would recognize me.

It was time. I wasn't really nervous, just very excited, and gave a quick shift to my clothes. As I walked up the driveway, I saw a young man going into the house and coming back out, carrying a box and throwing a duffle bag into the back of a truck. He was moving back and forth from the house to the truck.

There was someone coming down the driveway, and I recognized her as my mother. At the time of this dream she was still very much alive—but here she looked very different. She seemed spirit-like, ethereal. She was dressed in a familiar house dress of the 1960s, her brown hair was in soft curls against her peach-blushed skin—and she looked very much the young thirty-nine-year-old widow my father had left behind.

I could see that she was upset, a few tears lingered on her checks, but there was something else, too, and I couldn't quite read it—a bit of anger or resentment? No, that wasn't it. More like disbelief, because she was shaking her head slowly from side to side, like she was trying to grasp or understand something, or perhaps not really understanding at all.

I started toward her, but in this dream state she didn't notice me, then moments later she disappeared altogether.

What was it that my mother was having a hard time accepting? Theirs had been a romantic story of true love; tragically cut short, novel stuff, the love of her life suddenly gone, leaving her with five small children and few skills outside the home. She would spend the next forty years adapting to the changes his early death had brought upon her, and she had spent those years loving and waiting for him and their heavenly someday they would have together.

I continued walking up the driveway, more curious than ever, and up to the open tailgate of the older model truck. The young man was now inside the bed of the truck, busy arranging his gear. He was about twenty-one years old and wearing an army uniform. I stood there for a moment watching him.

I waited for a break in his attention, to ask if he knew the whereabouts of my father. But just as I was thinking the question, I heard a message and it was coming from the young man—in the form of telepathy, an exchange from soul to soul. I was made to know that it was he—this young man was my father! I was looking at a new extension of the man I had known and loved.

Nothing about him looked like my father as I took a hard look at him. His mouth was wider and full of bigger, pointier teeth than my Dad's. Although he was okay-looking, my father had been an extremely handsome man, with a full head of jet-black hair which he had worn slicked back with *Brylcreem*, a hair gel type product so popular in the fifties and sixties, and the little ditty of a song "a little dab will do ya" came to mind.

This young man's hair had a slight receding hairline and was closely buzzed, with just enough growth to see that it was a very light brown. The short style also revealed a tattoo near the top right side of his head, toward the forehead, an elongated triangle with some kind of a solid squiggle going through it. My father would *never* have gotten a tattoo; his brother, while in the navy, had put them on his arms and fingers as result of a good time at a port o'call, but was sorry after he returned home. He had to painstakingly cover them with long sleeves and bandages when at work, and my uncle suffered much embarrassment over his youthful decision. In those days, a tattoo could really hold you back. In the 1950s and 1960s, there was a lot of judgment on those sporting tattoos. My father had worked really hard to leave judgment and the life of a poor, homeless foster kid in his past.

My telepathic conversation with this young man continued: "I just met with your mother, he said, "and although my love for her is eternal, I need my all my energy for the work ahead. I'm going to war, and I'll need to focus on that alone." I knew he was asking the same of me, to let go of the father parted from this world for over forty-five years, but now here again as a young soldier.

He was a good man and would be a brave soldier, and it was impressed upon me that it was "important" for me to accept his "new incarnation."

Standing there in a kind of disbelief I wondered: Had he been on earth again for over twenty years? Breathing the same air as me for over twenty years? Why didn't I know it?

I began to scroll through my understanding of what I already knew of reincarnation. This was a lot for me to take in. Looking at this stranger whom I had once known as my dad. The young man never stopped the job of packing his gear during our exchange, as if the telepathic communication was not from him but from somewhere deep inside of him, from his soul to mine. I found myself just staring at him. His mannerisms were nothing like my father's.

Beginning to feel awkward just standing there, I tried to think of something to say, a way to say goodbye, but I was shaking and dizzy, knowing that my world and my understanding of it would never be the same. I felt a need to reach out to him, to compel him from his busy work and really look at me. He stopped immediately as if he'd heard my thoughts as they formed. He seemed to know what I needed and he looked directly at me.

The moments slowed between us, and I instinctively reached out toward his face. Then awkwardly I held myself back from touching him, trying to control the tightness that was forming deep in my throat, confused by all that I was seeing and hearing.

We held our gaze for only moments, until his tattoo distracted me. It was a strange marking on his head, and I felt an overwhelming need to touch it. Sensing this, he lowered his gaze as my finger lovingly traced its form. Something miraculous happened at the exact moment I touched his tattoo. I felt the spiritual essence of him and the totality of all he was.

The clearest of memories began to scroll past my eyes, a kaleidoscope of the many lives we had shared together, and many more that we had not racing through my mind. I watched the images play out, recognizing him over and over again. The scenes were in so many different lifetimes, so many different roles of earthly experience, and we had been the stars in uncountable lives together. This young man *was* the father I knew and loved. He was just in a different embodiment now.

Through our souls, I was made to understand that I would never lose him, that we were bonded in an eternal love for one another. The essence of my father was still here and always would be—and I was also made to know that I would always have access to the spiritual essence of him, the *father energy* that I missed so much.

The man I knew is in there, but this new body would have no memory of us. I am a part of his past, a life and a family of so many years ago. He was to move on and live anew, gaining a different experience and perspective.

I did not ask this young man for his name or anything of him. He was no longer tied to me here. It didn't matter. The physical nature of him was not tied to me, not in the here and now.

The energy of my father, of all of us, is enormous—too much to harness and contain within one human body. So it is portioned out, much of it to remain in the Afterlife, some of it to join in a new body and a new earthly existence, as I was shown.

My mind has been opened, and I want to learn as much as is allowed while here on earth, where the lessons are hard, but now with the knowledge that the experience stays with us for all of time.

I have read that many who experience a Near Death Experience, an NDE, are told that all that there is can be found in *Love and Knowledge*. That is what we get to keep when we pass over—that all that matters is *Love and Knowledge*.

I have accepted this very personal lesson in reincarnation, how better to understand it than by example, and what better example than within the deep love I hold for my father. Though gone from me for over forty-five years now, apparently after twenty-five years on the Other Side, he was ready to come back for a do-over.

I was gifted a meeting with him to further my understanding of spiritual workings—*We Come Back*! We are given another play, another character, another chance to perform. This gift, given by a loving God, assists us in experiencing all. Then we are welcomed back "home" to the Other Side—to share, merge, learn and teach from our experience.

It was time for me to leave, and we would take a step backwards and look at each other again as stranger to stranger. I gave a patriotic thank you for his service and wished him God Speed in battle.

I turned to leave this young soldier, with much more of an understanding of God than when I arrived. I left him knowing that although he and I no longer have a connection in my earthly life, we are and forever will be connected on the Other Side. The memories of our many lifetimes together will never be lost, for we are bound by a love beyond earthly understanding.

I would add here that I look forward to the many more lives we may share together. I sincerely hope for the chance—to one day, someday—just sit together under a big Oak tree on the Other Side. I would like a chance to share and experience the memory of my dad in this lifetime, and have an opportunity to sit in his lap once again and be his little girl. I want to smell his hair and feel his hands, and enjoy the safety and comfort just being next to him as I remember him in this lifetime.

I love you, Daddy, beyond words and worlds, always and forever.

~ ~ ~

A Warrior Revealed

I have long sensed a deeper side to my son Jesse. As a young child, he was deeply aware of his surroundings and had a strong sense of what was "fair." He always felt a need to correct the injustices of the world.

Though the growing-up years were sometimes filled with his own created strife, I *knew* that Jesse had a special internal struggle, that he is something of a rescuer, whether bringing home a stray cat or defending a child being bullied in a hallway at school. He has a "righter of wrongs" attitude, a defense usually accomplished with his fists.

As Jesse's parents, we grew weary of him being hauled into the principal's office to define the reason he had hit one of the bigger kids in the class. We also had a pride in him for doing so, though we hid our true feelings in order to discipline his behavior.

Jesse became known as a defender at school, also as one not to be messed with. He was not afraid of those who outsized him, and entered the arena with a sense of justice and strength in doing what he knew to be right, that somehow he would prevail, and the kids started to take notice. Even the principal began pardoning a bloodied nose or two, or four.

The pardon usually accompanied a promise of not to do it again, but we all knew that Jesse had a need within his soul to defend and to give voice to those meeker than he.

Eventually, he began strategically using an embarrassing remark about a bully—such as a certain bed-wetting incident during a sleep over or rejection of a girl at a dance—aimed directly at the bully to turn the situation around on them. A crowd would circle the perpetrator, pointing and laughing—bullying the bully, so to speak. Jesse would befriend the original target and the bully would learn a valuable lesson in how fickle a crowd can be, all willing to go along with the strongest voice.

I am proud to say that with Jesse's intolerance, bullying at his school dropped to an almost non-occurrence.

Now some twenty-plus years later, as I am lying in bed, it is the beginning of daylight and I have begun a morning ritual of stretching, yawning and dozing, savoring the last few moments before another day's beginning—when I hear *"Clou-dia."* This is not a misspelling of my name Claudia, but a purposeful mispronunciation of it. This was a christening by my spirit guide some months ago, at the beginning of our communications, a loving tease that always gets my immediate attention.

"CLOU-DIA, WAKE UP!"

I was now wide awake and sitting up on the edge of the bed, and I saw a type of white screen building itself in front of my eyes. I had been receiving visions on a more regular basis, so I wasn't afraid. I paid close attention to the screen, and a figure on it began to take shape, and a young male warrior appeared.

His facial position never moved as the images played out, as clear as if watching a movie; various landscapes, costumes, and scenarios would be shown as the man's face morphed into some new character. Each time, the eyes remained the same, but the hair color and style—long or curly, dark black or dirty blonde—would be different. Sometimes he would have a beard or a different shaped nose or chin.

He might be on horseback, or in a position to run; often his arm was extended, his hand holding something that also morphed—from a spear to a sword, or a raised fist ready for battle. Other times he held a muzzle-loading rifle, a dueling pistol, or a revolver.

All of the scenes transitioned from one to another without changing the exact position of his face. As I watched the clips unfold before me, I noticed the familiar eyes and unmistakable chiseled cheekbones of this warrior's face. I had to catch my breath as it came to me—*Jesse!* I was being shown countless versions of my son in the warrior role he has played for eons. Just as I was coming to this realization, I heard the word *mastodon,* and I knew this was right, too—that Jesse has filled this role from the beginning of his time here on Earth.

As this movie concluded and the screen faded away, I felt a broader confirmation of what I had always known of Jesse. *He is a righteous warrior and protector. That is who he is.* That is his Soul Contract and the role he has played many different times, in many different ways, in many different lives. He has a deep-seated knowing of his role in life, and he plays it well.

~ ~ ~

A 360-Degree View

In meditation and prayer I have been asking for more, not of this world, but for more pieces of and answers to the perpetual puzzles of the spiritual realm. I also seek guidance as to what is my part within it; as I slide further into my sixties, I really want to know that I am accomplishing my mission—the reason and purpose I am here. If not, I had better get to it!

I am aware of and excited by the progression I have made, the years of research by books, by dreams, by visions, by lessons, by service and life experiences, by good times and dark times, loneliness and joy, and the wonderful gifts of likeminded friends along my path.

I am so grateful for all I have received, and yet I find myself asking for more, a connection, a heavenly hello, an "Atta girl." Though I preface my asks with, "I don't need it, but I want it. Please, sir, can I please have some more"; at times, offering a zealous or pleading tone, "I want to know more, see more!" I pray to achieve the most of the experience this time around, and I do carry a feeling of being truly protected, nudged, and guided.

There is much fun in the mystery and connecting the dots, though dreams etc. can become an addicting game, played with loving guides who are willing to share what they feel I am ready to know and they are ready to help me—*If I ask.* For that is key in our Free Will Contract. Nothing is forced upon us, and there is no "right" path that we can fall from.

Our path is an intended lesson/experience of our own choosing—setting up the journey long before we arrived here. Who our parents are and the countries where we are born are well-orchestrated coincidences. Chance meetings in our lifetime, who we befriend or love, a charted life course, with willing soul participants taking on the starring roles, all worked out in advance. But this is not set in stone. All is subject to the free will we are given, to make our own choices.

Our course can be redirected, and this is the miraculous beauty of this earthly play we are participating in and the roles we have chosen. Adjustments can and will be accommodated, and the experience of our intent can still have a successful outcome.

Nudges and Flashpoints

Some of the nudges we receive are preplanned flags of recognition, such as a funny dance move or the crooked smile of a new acquaintance. Something just feels familiar and a *knowing* happens, like Deja Vu, and the feelings for this new dance partner quicken—and you almost immediately know that someday they will become your husband or wife. Or a certain house on a seemingly familiar street where you feel you must live could be one of the layers to build upon the pre-plan of your children's experience, and on and on and on.

It could keep you up nights trying to figure it all out, because now that we are here, we can't for the life of us remember what the plan was—and that dear reader, was another conscious choice we made *before* our arrival. We entered, and were born through, a veil of separation that created the amnesia of the grand nature of who we truly are, which seeds the human doubts and fears we must work through.

The unconditional love of our creator would not leave us here all alone, without help. So we come in with triggers, or points of reference and recognition for us, planted within us, for our own gentle pushes; and they were "set up" long before our physical birth, to affirm that we are indeed on course for our intended task.

These implanted *flashpoints* help to ignite and steer us—but never are our lives on autopilot, with a set destiny or outcome.

We Are Not Set Up to Fall

We are not set up to fail and fall from God's grace, to be punished for not having lived a perfect spiritual life here. That is what we came from—absolute perfection—but we were sent here to experience imperfection: security and fear, pleasure and pain, justice and injustice; these are only a small part of the dualities we face in this world.

Can we overcome hardships tossed our way with grace? Can we express love, show kindness and care for our fellow man in the midst of our own daily struggle for survival here?

We had a hand in setting up our own stumbling blocks along the road and what we can learn from each experience. Perhaps our personal knowledge will help another headed down the same path?

Can we move forward with a greater understanding of what it took to overcome our stumbles and move forward, living in appreciation of our accomplishments and sharing the fruits? Will stumbling blocks prove to be our stepping-stones along the road?

The Big Life Exam

Life is an examination, but it is not a test with right and wrong answers—only experiences from which we can learn. The evaluation that is to take place at the 360-degree review on the Other Side will be our own and of ourselves. Judgment and punishment is not the purpose of the exam, for that is a man-made concept. The self-evaluation will come from witnessing and reliving our experiences through the eyes of those who were affected by us, those whom we may not even realize or remember that we hurt. We will have the opportunity to feel those hurts and sorrows, and we will be mindful of their cause—that it was us and our actions that caused their distress, and that awareness of it will be admonishment enough.

There is also another perspective that we experience during the 360-degree view. It is all of the kindnesses we have shown, the helpful moments we created. We experience these, also, through the eyes of those we affected for the better.

How wonderful to be able to see the difference we made in someone's life by a simple gesture, one so seemingly small. We may not even remember the incident, but it created a deep impact on their life and those around them, just like throwing a stone into a stream and watching the ripples push outward, each ripple affecting the next, expanding and growing as it gains momentum.

There is much joy in the review as we witness these ripples and feel the positive experiences that we created while here.

The Theatre of Life Is a Gift

Be mindful that your life is a gift, and this *theatre of life* was created especially for you—by you and the spiritual advisors who love and know all of your strengths and weaknesses. The situations and players are poised to bring out the best and the worst of you.

There are many similarities to the holographic room in *Star Trek*. This masterfully crafted world of dualities was created with unconditional love for us and made especially for us, with an opportunity of choice to come back and play over and over again, each time a chance to experience something entirely new, the players and roles reversed, the centuries changed, even the gender switched for new perspectives and experiences.

We will realize our greatest enemies here on Earth are our closest confidants and friends from the Other Side, having played their part so well they brought us to our knees in grief and pain in order for us to grow. After our earthly deaths, we will embrace each other with a pat on the back of a job well-done, because with our spiritual eyes we'll see and understand, and we'll say, "Bravo friend, well played!"

Earth Life Theatre

I include a picture below of the life theatre as it was shown to me in Spirit School. It is arched, like an amphitheater:

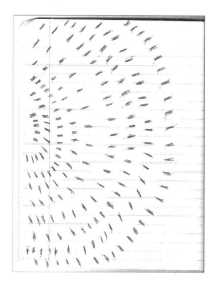

The starring roles are represented in the small half circle; the handful of closest family, friends and lovers who will make their mark in our world for good and bad and will play the intricate roles of longevity in our life arena. The rings continue outward, each a smaller role than the last—but all are important. Even the last rows, the cheap seats, the walk-on players with small one-line parts cannot be measured by a lesser degree of impact, because they represent vehicles that can touch our lives or change its direction.

I am in awe of the love shown us by our Higher Source—Maker, God, Creator—of this and the many untold worlds that were created for us to experience, grow and learn. That is our precious gift, and as we play, we learn, for there is no greater way to learn than by actual experiences.

I am in gratitude of the love shown us by the magnanimous undertaking of the creation of this beautiful physical world, and the opportunity to experience all of it, in a 360-degree continuation of lessons that are carried back within us through the veil upon our physical death, to be shared with our Maker.

We are here so that God can experience His own imagination.

~ ~ ~

A Dog's Purpose, A Grandmother's Purpose

Yesterday, I had a movie date with my seven-year-old grandson Jude. I was watching the clock, waiting for him, parked near the front door of his school.

At the sound of the bell, I watched for his head full of blond hair and looked for his face among the sea of children exiting as they all ran, searching for their parents' cars in the crowd of waiting vehicles, engines on, heaters blaring. It was cold, this last day of January, and all these little bodies were creating their own heat as breath turned to steamy mist as they ran.

Jude and I spotted each other at almost the same time, his excited little hand waving as he ran toward me, the beaming smile on his face as he called out, "Grandma!" This recognition brings my heart an overflowing joy. These little ones who call me Grandma are a beautiful gift that age and children give, and it makes all the gray hair and wrinkles worthwhile.

As he got into the car, he began a five-minute repartee of his day: the pencil he was given that changes colors when either warm or cold, a classmate's daddy who is a policeman came to see them and even showed them the *REAL* gun he wears on his belt, the spelling test where he only missed one word, but I fail to remember which word because he immediately jumped into his story of accidentally bumping into a kindergartener and his nose absorbed the brunt of the blow and he had to go to the nurse's office for an ice pack. All this spilled out as he buckled himself into the backseat.

I turned to take a good look at his nose and noticed the crayon-colored crown he was wearing and asked him about it, did it have a special meaning.

"No, Grandma. I just made it."

Then as I checked the rearview mirrors for departure, he became excited about something new. "Grandma, ever since I first opened my eyes and saw it was today, I've been waiting for our movie date together."

This made my heart swell.

He quickly added: You are my bestest, prettiest grandma and I love you sooo much, did you know that?"

I could hardly swallow the lump in my throat, as I smiled at this blue-eyed marvel. "I love you too, sweet man."

We spent time at McDonalds, a quick hamburger, the climbing wall of blue and green plastic rocks, each making a musical noise. Jude scaled ever upward, then slid down for another sip of soda or a quick look at his happy meal toy figure.

It was time to leave for the movie and we had decided together to see *A Dog's Purpose,* the story of a boy and his beloved dog, except this dog continued to reincarnate, he would die then be born again into another dog body—but never losing himself, he always had the same mind and retained the love of his past owners, collecting memories with new experiences and new owners.

It's an amazing film—the cinematography, the background music, the acting, the pleasing voice and dialogue of the dog, not too young or kiddy-like. Adults and kids alike were glued to the movie screen, laughing aloud. I took repeated peeks at Jude's face as he watched. He didn't move, his hand still holding onto an unopened candy bar. He was fixated. I watched for signs of confusion or if the dog's death might bring nightmares, but my fears seemed unfounded as he laughed at some scenes or was quiet and calm in the sadder scenes.

As the movie drew to a close, I looked at the audience around us. People were smiling, as they wiped away tears. Its message was powerful.

Jude was not crying, and he said aloud, "Wow, Grandma! That was the greatest movie I ever saw!" As we walked to the car, we talked about its meaning. I wondered if he had really understood.

He started with, "Now I get it. The dog kept coming back over and over after he died so he could to get back to Ethan!"

"That's right." And I asked him, "Do you think that could really happen? Do you think people could do it, too?"

Jude slowed his pace, giving this a great deal of thought. Then he stopped and looked up at me. "I don't know why not. It would be good if you never really died and you got to keep your same mind and come back and keep learning new things. Why not keep coming back? Why couldn't it be real?"

Astounding for a seven-year-old, I thought, but then not for Jude. I had long recognized his ability for deeper thinking. He would study a situation and ponder, and he wasn't afraid to ask intelligent questions beyond his young years, expecting real answers and discussion.

I loved his acceptance of there being a real a possibility of this newly introduced theory of reincarnation, and it filled me with a pride beyond words that he and I could converse on a another level of understanding and friendship.

"I'm proud of your 'deep thinking'."

"Yes, Grandma" he said "We are both deep thinkers, aren't' we?"

I bent down and hugged him, as that familiar lump swelled in my throat "Yes, we are, my sweetest little man. Yes, we are."

~ ~ ~

Grub Love

After years of research, prayers and meditation, I began to have very detailed dreams of encountering myself in various forms. I suppose the student was ready, because the floodgates opened and for months my dreams were filled with many versions of myself living very different lives.

I have lived as an entirely different gender and race, than the woman I am now; and in many time periods and cultures, teeming with very different conditions, situations and struggles. I have been made aware that all were gifted opportunities, each a chance to experience living in the physical and the objective of gaining new perspectives by each experience.

Many of these dream-experiences either ended or began with me—this Claudia—standing in front of a mirror or a still body of water and seeing a very different person looking back. The mirror images, witnessed through my own eyes, have helped in my gradual acceptance and understanding that I was indeed truly looking at myself as someone else but still very much *me*.

I have accepted more than just the possibility of reincarnation or the act of coming back into a physical existence again and again, as I now have a doubtless knowing of this to be so. I have come back again, not in the sense of trying to "get it right" or of being trapped in a karmic state of do-over, but rather as a loving gift of opportunity to grow and learn from each experience. What better way to understand or empathize with others than through having walked in their shoes, so to speak? This is our gateway to a true acceptance of one another and advancement in the nurturing of an unconditional love for each other.

Last night's dream-experience was no different than the others except that the scene began in total darkness. I had no sense of sight. I was completely blind. But it didn't matter. All other senses were heightened and everything in this world was about feeling and the feeling was of complete comfort and bliss. My existence was delightful, and I was so very happy, I would have stayed there forever, but this is where my lesson was to begin, and the question of where I was, and who I was, and what I was to learn.

As I was feeling and thinking this, a light came on in the warm darkness—and I was able to view the scene from outside the perspective of Claudia. I saw that I was *not* alone in the darkness.

Rather, I was part of a group or colony and all were my compadres. There was no distinction between us, no need for titles, or labels. All here were the same. We were family, friends, lovers, brothers and sisters, neighbors. And we all lived against, next to and on top of each other, all clustered together. We didn't know anything but the warmth and comfort of each other in our shared home of fertile soil and moist darkness. Our survival was of a universal mind. We ate, had sex, slept, inched into a new spot, had more sex and ate again, and slept, we were all together and with each other, and it was wonderful.

When I woke, having spent the night reliving a life lived in the soil within a colony of lowly garden grubs, I could have been grossed out, but I wasn't. I realized I had been given a valuable perspective of life in all forms: that none is more relevant than another, that no level of life is more superior to another.

This firsthand knowledge kindled an understanding and appreciation of a simplistic way to live a happy, contented, and blissful life. In fact, as I think about it, of all of the lives I have recalled living before, this grub life is one of the most satisfying in terms of contentment ... and warm fuzzies, pun intended.

~ ~ ~

~ ~ ~

Awaiting Feeling

We await a perfect monumental moment
taking perception to untouchable status
every breathtaking impulse swallowed and surfing
dodging strenuous danger brought upon through
unnecessary suffering of society's furious outtakes
we escape and leave unfollowed paths
create destiny spiritually indulged
heaven a gift everlasting peace
if never fallen from grace.

~ Aaron Joseph Clayton

~ ~ ~

9
Dreams

Be a Disciple to Thyself

~ ~ ~

The Gift of Dreams and Keeping a Dream Journal

While still living in Colorado, I would often visit my family in Salt Lake City, and enjoyed my stays in my son Aaron's home. This allowed me to spend good quantity time with my young grandson. Though only three years old, he uses an adult vocabulary and has the depth, in thought, of an old soul. Needless to say, we get along great.

These overnight stays allow me to see Jude first thing in the morning, wearing fuzzy jammies and a sleepy face. I give him a squeeze, and then ask him, "Did you have happy dreams?"

"HAPPY DREAMS!" is always his retort. I'm glad that his dreams are happy, though he is never able to tell me what happened in them.

My husband has a hard time recalling his dreams as well, and I find this sad, as so much goes on when you are relaxed, having allowed the stress of the day to slide away and the unconscious you is set free. It is all allowed out to be examined and explored. This can give a huge insight into what is going on inside your own head. In our dreams, we are aware of much more than in our waking hours. It is also the time for deep spiritual communication, when our higher self and guides can nudge us back onto our path, or deliver information and messages directly to our soul.

Let yourself dream. Then try to recall at least one detail of it upon waking, before the new day rushes in.

This requires practice—to just lie still, just for a few moments, with your eyes closed.

Your dreams can be recalled by the feeling that lingers, or remembering who else was in the dream, how old you were in the dream, or what were you wearing. Sometimes, even going through a list of colors in your mind can spark a memory of the night's most recent dream, as color evokes emotion.

For example, I ask myself, did it feel yellow or purple? Sometimes, a dream comes back to me by examining colors as a stimulus.

Recalling, then working to analyze your dreams, will help you gain valuable insight into yourself.

As I am going through my own spiritual metamorphous of late, my dreams have become an integral part of my education of myself. I welcome communication with my guides ... especially their gentle nudges or affirmations that things are okay.

Then there are the best dreams—my favorites—the visits from my loved ones who have passed. Though these dreams are few and far between, I cherish them.

~ ~ ~

"It's All Going to Be OK," she said. "You're Going to Be Alright."

I was going through some turbulent times in my life about fifteen years ago, questioning the choices I had made, where I was going, what I was doing, where did I belong, and who did I belong with. You know, some of the good "queries" we sometimes go through in this life.

My grandmother came to me in a dream. She looked wonderful

and youthful. Her hair no longer carried the gray of old age but was the soft light brown of her younger years.

She was sitting on a huge rock in the middle of a fast-moving stream. I wanted to run to her as soon as I recognized her, but the rushing waters kept me at bay. I darted about looking for a way to get to her, as she calmly sat, looking comfortable, and completely dry.

Her head was tilted back, her face lifted to the sun. She was simply glowing, and I could see that she was smiling. Her simple dress was pulled up over her knees, her feet dangling in the cool water. I was so happy to see her! Though gone from me now over forty years, I loved her still and had always been so proud of her. I grew up admiring her strength and ability to persevere through the hardships she had faced in her lifetime, yet her heart was soft and loving, and she was happy and kind.

She had widowed early, left alone to care for nine small children, and the farm they worked so hard to keep was lost in the Great Depression. These were only a few of the adversities she faced in her life here as Anna Mildred Hall Strong.

I was frustrated by the rushing water that separated us, and continued to look for an entry and the possibility of stones to step onto and move myself closer to her.

She slowly turned and smiled at me.

I extended my arms out to her, reaching only the air between us. "Grandma!" I called out. "Grandma!" I waved, but I was unsure if she could hear me over the water's rush.

Then I heard her. Her voice was calm and smooth, and she wasn't yelling over the racing water. Her voice was being carried through it, and not muffled but soft and clear as a bell: "It's all going to be okay," she said. "You're going to be alright." I woke, but calmly lay in the dark, recalling the details of her face, her hair, and the way she was dressed. This was all captured in a memory that I would hold close to my heart, and the sound and softness in the tone of her voice, without a trace of worry or unrest, and the clarity of its delivery. She was telling me that I was going to be all right, and that I would get through this hard time. It was all going to be ok, and I believed her.

~ ~ ~

"Did You Do Your Best?"

I had the most vivid dream the other night. It has stayed with me, or should I say I have kept it with me and will forever, because of its content.

My dad passed away over forty years ago. I was sixteen. I have missed him so very much and although, at times, I have felt his presence and protection through all of these years, I had wanted, begged, and prayed for a dream of him. I wanted to see him again so I could remember the way he moved, the way he tilted his head when he smiled, the great way he smelled, and to feel the warmth of his hug and the touch of his strong hands. Most of all, I wanted to hear his voice, as the sound of it had faded over so many years without hearing it. I wanted to have my dad again, even for a few brief moments in a dream. That was my want, my hope and, if a Genie were to somehow grant me three wishes, it was at the top of my list!

Why had I not dreamed of him in all of these years? Words here cannot express my frustration as the memory of him faded. *Please let me dream of him so I won't forget,* became my mantra.

THANK YOU! THANK YOU! THANK YOU! My dream, it came! I got my dream!

Sleep that night was no different than any other, except somewhere in the misty blackness, I found myself walking on a path. I was surrounded by many of my friends and acquaintances. Three that stood out to me were Dawn, Robyn and Brook, so much a part of me in my younger years, and all are so dear to me still.

They were lined up on either side of where I walked, they were so happy for me, and cheered me forward. As I passed by them, I was able to feel each one's individual support and well wishes—but I looked only straight ahead because now the path was changing, it was climbing upward and toward something, and I was drawn to it, moving forward, though I could not yet see what lay ahead.

As I drew closer to the end of the path, I saw him. My dad! He was sitting in a big comfy overstuffed yellow chair. I could see his dark hair with graying temples and his big crooked smile, and I could feel the inviting warmth that came from it! His eyes sparkled as he saw me, too, and I moved faster now, my smile even larger than his. Almost running now, soon I would be right in front of him.

When at last I stood before him, I could not contain my joy! I wanted to say so many things, like where have you been for so long? I wanted to tell him how much I had missed him. But before my happy ramblings could begin, he suddenly became very serious and his smile evened out, and I felt halted before I could reach out to him.

Then in his most serious fatherly voice, he asked me, "Did You Do Your Best?"

As a kid, I had heard this question many times. A lot of Daddy/daughter time was spent going over my report cards and term papers, with less than stellar achievement and a note needing to be signed by my parents. This always meant a talking-to, which always led to the question, "Did you do your best?" I usually replied, "Yes," because I was a kid and that's what kids say, although in my heart I knew I could have done better.

Now I was standing in front of my father after so many years apart, in this dream state of being both an adult woman and his sixteen-year-old daughter, answering this most serious life question posed to me by my father, whom I admired and loved.

I took a small step backward, a little miffed that my happiness to see him was resulting in a feeling of being in trouble, and I was getting a talking to. I took a moment before I answered as a confident adult. "Yes Dad, I Did", adding, "It's really hard down there, and I admit that I have made some mistakes, but Dad I've tried really hard and I really have done my best."

As my eyes welled and tears begin to flow, my dad reached out to me and pulled me onto his lap. My cheek brushed against his familiar scratchy whiskers, I nuzzled up to his face—the smell of him, the color of his khaki pants, texture of his shirt, the sound of his voice, his hands so large and strong as they held mine. All my senses were filled. This sixty-year-old little girl was in her daddy's arms once more and all of the time apart from him was melting away.

I awoke knowing that I had spent the entire night there, talking to him, but I can remember nothing more of our conversation. What I do remember is more than enough to know that he is still a part of me and that he was pleased with my answer.

"Yes, Dad, it's really hard down there but, Dad, I really have done my best."

~ ~ ~

Don't Panic

I was recently struck by a post in a Facebook group site I belong to, placed there by a talented intuitive and seeker. RW is a member with whom I have felt akin in many of her insights.

She posted within the group's face book page, about *seeing* BIG WORDS in her dreams, like the ones I see. The most recent ones shown to her were: DON'T PANIC. She was equating seeing these words to a book she was reading at the time, *The Hitch Hikers Guide to the Galaxy.*

As she and I e-chatted, each replying to one another's new insights, we shared the words that were showing up in our dreams. She said that she *knew* the meanings of the words she was seeing, adding that one members interpretation did not feel 'right' to her. This was a valuable lesson in *following your own feelings* when trying to interpret what your dreams mean.

Dreams are sent to us by our guides, and the meanings and messages are meant specifically for us. So, *you* are the best one to interpret what your own dreams mean, as these messages are accompanied with a *feeling*, to assist in your interpretation. So, trust your own abilities. Trust your own feelings.

The conversation continued, as a comment made by another

person in the group, gave the following example. While sitting with his child watching cartoons one morning, he realized that he understood his own message as he watched a scene of a snowball rolling downhill. As the ball picked up momentum, growing larger as it rolled on and on, he realized that this scene was something he had dreamed a few nights before—about a problem he was having. And now he was watching this same scenario in animated form on TV.

I feel that his story was my own guide chiming in, because I too had a similar dream a few nights later. I was standing on a level spot at the top of a steep hill next to a large snowball that I had been rolling. Inside this big ball of snow-packed ice, I could clearly see two words: *Chaos* and *Distress*. In the dream, I had managed to roll them both inside of this ball, holding it under control, as it was poised to roll downward. Although all was level now, if I kept pushing the ball forward, it would pick up speed on its own and grow larger and larger. By the time it reached the bottom of the hill, I would have lost all control.

I stood there feeling that I had a choice. Rather, that *I* had been making a choice all along, controlling, and managing the chaos and distress in my own life. Now, I realized that I could give it a heave hoe. I didn't need to let my own distress roll out of control, nor did I need to hang onto it forever trying to balance and control it. I could make the decision to let it go.

I awoke giggling—*clever guide*—I have learned to enjoy the comedic spin he attaches to my lessons.

Life throws chaotic days our way every now and again, for whatever reason; test, lesson, amusement, or just plain happenstance. It just happens sometimes no matter how well planned our days are—this is the nature of life.

So, expect a bit of chaos to keep you on your toes; roll with it, and then let it go.

You Should Stick Around; Browse Even

In the beginning of the final chapter of my mother's life, she called me one afternoon with barely enough breath to speak. "Claudia, I don't feel very good," she whispered into the phone.

I dropped everything to get to her side quickly, a silent alarm in my heart of this woman who never complained, her nickname the "energizer bunny."

This declaration of hers was huge evidence that we were entering her final stage. She was still living in her home, this place that she and my father had purchased in 1957, paid for in ten years by scrimping, saving and working vigilantly toward the end goal of burning the mortgage due, by adding two extra principle payments with every month's payment.

Now, as I entered the only home my mother had known for almost sixty years, I knew immediately that if I didn't take her to the hospital right now she would soon pass in her own bed. I asked her directly what her preference was. I gave her assurance that I would stay by her side through it all, whether it be in her own home or the hospital, adding that if she left, she may not ever be well enough to return.

She had made the decision that she did not want her home to be stigmatized, and she felt it would be harder for all of us left behind if she passed at home, so we raced to the hospital.

This story could be wrapped around hospital procedures and modern-day miracles but that is not the story that I have to tell here.

My mother did not pass that evening, and after a few days in the hospital ICU she seemed suspended in a catch 22, not getting any better, not getting any worse. I stayed with her as promised.

The third night at the hospital, I had the first of several prophetic dreams of the difference between God time and earth time. I dreamed that my mother and I were walking down an eclectic, artsy street full of cute local shops. We were having one of our travel adventures together, laughing and enjoying each other's company, when we spotted an old-fashioned candy store, complete with a huge pink awning hung over the front window and we just had to go inside.

We were awkwardly alone for a few moments before a sales lady came out from behind boldly patterned curtains. They were radiant, but not nearly as colorful as the woman who stepped through them. She was very short and heavyset, with the darkest black hair pulled into a topknot, and accentuated by a pencil sticking through it. Her face seemed pinched under thick, black cat-woman eyeglasses, with beaded chains draping down to her apron, her hands on her hips. Her cheeks were heavily dotted with rouge, and her lips pursed outward in a fishlike pucker; revealing crooked teeth behind a thick layer of candy-apple-red lipstick.

Her booming voice and appearance startled us as she spoke in a tough-as-nails New York accent, "Come in. Come in. Look around and find whatever you want." She was a perfect human version of Roz in Disney's movie *Monsters Inc.,* her deep gravelly voice coming from somewhere deep within her throat.

"Sometimes it can take *forever*," she said, accentuating *forever*.

We told her we had come in already knowing what we wanted, and she took a long pause as she sized us up, chewing on an oversized wad of gum, her jaw working overtime between repetitive popping.

"Oh, browse awhile," she said. "Take your time. These things can sometimes take forever. Stay awhile. Browse even."

She didn't want to accept that our minds were already made up.

I woke feeling strongly that I had received a prophetic message from my guide, dressed up in this memorable character, the message being that were to have an unforgettable experience together with this hospital stay and that, although we thought we already knew what the outcome would be, we were being strongly encouraged to slow down and take in the moments. As I realized this, I knew that our last adventure together wasn't to be over as quickly as we thought.

There is timing in everything, and a time to every purpose, under Heaven. I enjoyed my mother's sweet company for another two weeks, nights and days in that ICU hospital room, time together I would not trade for anything. We found things to laugh about in the midst of the loud hospital staff, who used the night hours to repair doors, lights and alarms; and she was given a chance for final visits and goodbyes with her beloved family.

She and I were punchy from exhaustion, and we both easily slipped into hazy dream states. I asked her several times if she had dreams of anyone coming to her in her sleep, had she seen my father or sister yet?

She said she had not, and from my years as a hospice volunteer, I knew that many spend days hovering between worlds. But my mom said she wasn't having any special dreams. Then she laughed, adding that maybe it was because she hadn't slept since being admitted. Quite possibly she was right, but one night I woke to find that she did indeed have a visitation.

~~~

The Tall One

I woke in the middle of the night in my mother's hospital room. I was in the nook of the large picture window with a pillow and blanket. After a few hours rest, I was now wide-awake.

A magical scene was taking place at the foot of her bed: Three floating orbs at the left side of my mother's bed, looking like unraveling balls of twine but they were golden electric energy, floating four feet in the air. Standing directly at the foot of the bed was a woman over seven feet tall, with flowing long brown hair. Her clothing was layers and layers of muted colored linens, as in biblical times.

Hardly believing my eyes and holding my breath as I watched, I blinked several times to make sure I was truly awake. Yes, I was. I continued to watch as the woman administered to my mother as I silently watched the amazing scene, afraid to move so I would not interrupt what was happening. I was so very happy that I was allowed to witness this!

This scene went on for about twenty seconds before all faded and

I was left in awe of what I had seen, in the middle of the night, at the foot of my mother's hospital bed.

My mother passed several days later, and I wondered about the grand figure that had come to her side to bring her aide. Was this in preparation for the transition she was soon to make?

I only know for sure that I witnessed a sacred scene of one of God's angels, accompanied by loving orbs of light, in service.

~ ~ ~

~ ~ ~

The Words You Are Given Are Yours To Use

~ ~ ~

10
Messages from the Other Side

~ ~ ~

Communication Via Text Message from my Mother—Who Never Owned a Cell Phone

I was deep into a texting conversation with my daughter-in-law, planning Thanksgiving dinner. It was a when, where, and who-would-bring-what kind of dialogue that was needed now that our beloved G'ma had passed away. It would be our first holiday without my mom and the familiar traditions she had established so long ago. The baton had been passed to me and I was nervously trying to hang onto what I could of the old traditions, as well as create some new traditions of my own.

The newest of traditions was to be a breakfast quiche with champagne and mimosas for family members who wouldn't be able to attend the main event later that afternoon. Gma didn't drink alcohol so, out of respect for her, none of us who did drink ever had at her home. This year was really going to be a different experience.

Our text messages were pinging back and forth, and I had just typed "mimosa and champagne etc. in the morning," when the keystrokes suddenly halted—until a full sentence appeared on the screen, and it was one that *I DID NOT TYPE*.

In the midst of the planning and reconstructing a day traditionally cooked and shared at Mom's home, I had no doubt who this message was from—but how on earth did she do this? She had never even owned a cell phone, let alone had ever sent a text message. But there it was, as plain as any other text message I had ever received. But this one from beyond this earthly realm: *"The bodies may die, but the love never does......<3"*

I screamed out for my husband. "Chris!" He had to witness this. "Bring your phone! Bring your phone!" I yelled, afraid the message would fade away before he would get here. "Hurry! Hurry! Take a picture of my screen!"

He captured the message! Proof! Clearly written. And it stayed there, on my screen. The picture below is the picture he took of my phone and the actual message I received that day, a heavenly message, a reminder and proof of the life that goes on after physical death, that the physical body is all that dies and that love *never* does.

Thank you, Mom, for a brilliantly delivered physical message that can be seen and shared! Obviously, you've been taking tech lessons on the Other Side!

Note: in preparing artwork for the book, an attempt was made in recreating this picture for a higher quality printing, but it was impossible to recreate. The phone would over ride any attempt to put 'morningthe' without a space between the words in the copy. In addition the messages (2) Clayton would not come up again, every attempt to make it read the same failed. I mean, you just can't override or improve a message from Heaven! ☺

~ ~ ~

Hello, Can You Hear Me, Now?

It has been almost a year since my mother passed, and the daily phone calls to check on her health are no longer needed. I have accepted that. There are times though when something happens in my life, times when I really want to share something good or maybe some bad news, or just to connect with her and hear her voice and laughter, and it has been hard to get used to her absence.

There are still times when I reach for the phone with the intent to call her, realizing that her familiar voice will not be answering me on the other end of the line. There will be no more hellos, and whatcha doings? And it just brings on an empty feeling akin to an amputee with a lost limb. It can still be felt but is just not there anymore.

I had a dream-experience of my mom the other night. We were on the phone together. I could see that she was holding a mobile phone to her ear, but noticed that it was one of the first of its kind, called the "brick" because of its large, heavy size. A really old-school model, it was white and had a hard, thick, six-inch rubber antenna sticking out the top of it.

Our conversation was not out of the ordinary, just a mother and daughter chatting as friends. However, during our conversation, in the dream I needed to quickly run into the other room for something. But my phone was still attached by a cord, so I sat it down and talked very loudly, in the hope that she could still hear me.

When I came back and picked up the phone, I asked if she had still been able to hear me. "Yes," she said, but then the tone in her voice changed. It became more pronounced and serious and she began to talk to me like a teacher, and I knew I was to pay close attention to her words.

She told me there was a button on the underside of the phone that most people never even know is there or pay any attention to. She continued, "You really have to look for it, and once you find it, you have to practice using it. If you do this, and if you really pay attention and listen, you will be able to hear me from a great distance." She added, "I may not sound exactly the same, but you will still be able to hear me and you will know that it is me."

The dream ended there, but it left me so happy. I had received a very real visit from my mother, who was still trying to teach me valuable lessons, now from the Other Side.

I woke with complete confidence that she is still listening, and that there will still be times ahead that we will connect and I will be able to hear what she is saying.

~ ~ ~

Affirmation Hot Sauce

The other day, I decided it was time to clean up the voicemails long stored in my phone, as it was teetering between almost full or completely full whenever I neglected to delete the one extra spot for new voice messages.

It had been this way for over a year, and it wasn't a good business practice for my busy real estate career—but you see, my phone holds many of my mother's phone call messages. As her health declined, I began to save them—and now that she had passed, how could I decide which ones were less precious than the others, so I had not deleted any of them.

I knew the inevitable would come one day when I would just need to hear her voice again. The recorded messages contained many simple "Whatcha doin's" and "call ya laters" and my favorite, the one that came early one morning when she sang the Happy Birthday song to me, adding her own words "Precious Claudia." to the lyrics. This recording is a most-treasured gift. How devastated I would be if I accidently deleted it, or lost my phone.

So I investigated what I could do to save them all ... and was elated to discover a way to safely take them off my phone and store them on my computer. As I did this, I listened to each one several times—which created a heavy mood of melancholy. I so missed our frequent calls to each other and wished I could pick up the phone for another of our mother/daughter conversations.

"I miss you, Mom!" I said aloud and started crying, and looked upward into the nothingness of my office ceiling.

Needing to take a break, I wiped my tears and went in to the kitchen to heat up a leftover burrito. As I waited for the familiar ding of the microwave, I pulled out a plate and a couple of Taco Bell hot sauce packets, and turned to get a fork from another drawer.

When I came back around, my attention was drawn to the sauce packets sitting side by side; they had small notes printed on them that I'd never noticed before, and the two packets laying next to one another contained a timely message:

Call your mom and...I missed you!

Wow. How had I missed seeing these printed words on these packets before?

I got out the plastic container where I put all manner of unopened ketchup and soy sauce packets that have been collected over the years and began to go through them, reading them all. There were messages on all the remaining hot sauce packets—but none that leapt into view at this timely moment—like *Call your mom* or *I missed you*!

Serendipity, synchronicity, or chance? Perhaps just a woman looking for something to hold onto in the midst of grieving her mother's loss? When we allow ourselves to remain open to the splendor and magic of the Universe, when we need it most we may receive a timely message in the oddest and most beautiful of ways.

~~~

A Sign from My Father

I was sixteen when my dad went to work one August morning in 1969. It was one of only a handful of mornings that I lingered in bed, not bothering to get up to say goodbye. It was summer and I was sleeping in.

The day was typical and routine, until mid-afternoon. Then everything in my life suddenly changed.

My dad, my father, my daddy was gone and was never coming home again. A tragic workplace accident up heaved the ordinary lives of his wife, five children, and even Tiny, our little white Chihuahua—who sadly spent the rest of his years laying at the end of the driveway, looking down the street, and waiting for the familiar sounds of the old Ford truck that would never bring him back.

I'm in my sixties now and not one day has passed in all of these years that my father's memory hasn't brushed through my mind in one way or another. I have often found myself looking for evidence of his continued existence, asking, "Where had he gone? Was he okay? Was he on the Other Side, and where was that? What was he doing? Did he see me? Did he remember me? Did he miss me, too?"

After so many years without my father, every now and again I thought I felt him near—but was he really? Was I merely imagining this from my own need?

Several years before I had experienced any dreams of my father, I decided to bake some cookies. I found myself struggling to perform this simplest of tasks. First, looking for the right measuring cup, thinking I had set it out but unable to find it—then, knowing I had taken out four eggs, but now I could only see three.

It was a blistery cold winters day, one not to be driving in, and I slipped on my coat and made my way to a neighbor's to borrow an egg, but no one answered. So I returned home, got back to the business of cookie dough—and saw the missing egg on the counter. *It*

98

must have rolled behind the bowl, I thought, trying to convince myself that I wasn't going crazy.

I picked up the egg to crack it into the bowl, but it slipped from my hand and I watched it fall, as if in slow motion comedic satire, and then splatter on the floor and my shoes. I stood over the mess and recounted the trouble this one little egg had caused.

Suddenly a warm feeling flooded through me and I laughed out loud," Dad? "Is that you, Dad? Are you here? Are you playing tricks on me?"

As a teenager, I had been an easy mark for teasing and my dad had often pulled pranks on me to get me out of my serious hormone-driven moods. He would move things, hide the hairbrush I'd pulled from the bathroom drawer only minutes before, move my lip gloss from my dresser and I would later find it on top a stack of books—all of which were turned in different directions. These little irritations would make me want to yell, until I'd hear him giggling from the other side of the room. He was just playing with me and trying to get my attention.

Now as an adult, fumbling with simple tasks and the elusive egg in my own kitchen, I had an overwhelming feeling I was being pranked, and I just 'knew' who the culprit was. The feeling of my dad was so strong that I phoned and told my mother, "I think Dad was with me today." Then I called and told my sister Kaylyn as well. They both indulged me as I expressed what I *felt* to be real.

Yet during each conversation, I still found myself searching for the truth of my experience, because all I really had to go on was my gut feeling, no scientific proof. *Was Dad really here?* I wondered. I juggled both the lightness of the feeling and the heaviness of the doubt, until I eventually let it go.

Three years after the disappearing-egg morning, my life was moving at a rapid pace. My precious only sister, my childhood partner in crime, the one with whom I shared my innermost thoughts and feelings, had died this spring.

Now it was autumn and I was so lonely for her. I needed her, and wanted to talk with her. So I decided to attend a metaphysical fair in

Colorado Springs and find a psychic or medium that might help me connect with her.

I had never done anything like this before, so I asked God to please show me some kind of a sign if this was a good idea, should I or not?

I read the advertisement again, noting that a twenty-minute reading was twenty dollars, and I decided I would go and just look around. I slipped into my jeans ... and found a forgotten crinkled twenty-dollar bill tucked into the front pocket. I had my sign of approval.

As I drove downtown, my expectations of a connection with my sister began to rise.

At the fair, I stopped by the booth of Reverend Janet Day, a clairvoyant well known in Colorado Springs. She was meeting with someone else when I approached her booth. Even so, she waved for me to sit and assured me she would be with me shortly. I took a chair and, while waiting, I tried to do some of my own connecting. I prayed that my sister would find a way to communicate with me. I prayed for my father to join in the conversation, too. I would be so happy to hear from either of them.

But my sister had been gone only a few months, and my dad now over forty years. Given the different times of their passing, I thought that my sister might be easier to reach, closer to earth, having just left it, this made some sense to me.

When my turn came, I sat across the table from Janet and she took my hands into hers. All she asked was for my own full name and she closed her eyes and became very quiet.

After a few moments, she told me that she sensed a "younger male energy" around me, but I didn't know any young men who had died. I looked at her and waited for more information, silently begging for female energy.

"Does this resonate with you?" Janet asked.

"No," I answered calmly, defying the urge to speak more strongly. "This isn't resonating with me at all." I had no cousins, brothers, or sons who had passed.

"His energy is very strong," Janet continued, her eyes still closed.

"He is behind you, leaning forward toward your left." She giggled at that. "He is very mischievous in nature. He kind of pops up from behind you, then to your left side."

I was speechless, listening to a bunch of stuff that wasn't making any sense to me at all.

"Now, he is showing me balloons, lots of different kinds of balloons, and the color blue is very prominent, a light turquoise blue." She went on saying, "The balloons are like hot-air balloons. Does any of this resonate with you?"

I took in a deep breath, trying to hold onto the last ray of hope I had that this would work. I gave her a confused, softly spoken reply. "No."

I started to feel a deep disappointment, as if the air was being released from a balloon, my balloon, the happy one I had come in with, so full of hope, now slowly deflating, the expectation of a connection beginning to sag. My thoughts screamed, *I don't know of any young male! FEMALE ENERGY, PLEASE! No young male energy, no balloons. I don't even really like the color turquoise blue!*

"Do you have a blue picture frame?" she asked. "He is showing me something blue with a bunch of balloons on it? I also see a patch of red on a balloon, like a big hot-air balloon."

"No," I answered, thinking, *Wow, she is really reaching now,* and I began to listen half-heartedly.

"His energy is strong *and* mischievous," she said again.

My expression showed that I had no recognition of this at all.

Frustrated that her information wasn't making sense, she conceded. "Perhaps I'm getting information meant for someone else. This doesn't happen often, but there are a lot of people in here."

I was so frustrated now, because I knew that my time was almost up. I asked if she could please ask the young male energy to step back, to see if anyone else was there to talk with me. Where was my sister? I wondered. Was this young male energy blocking her?

Then Janet asked, "Has your father died?"

I nodded.

"Could this be your father?"

This was a good question. I hadn't considered how young my

father was when he passed, and I was a girl in my teens, now fifty-nine. My dad would have been barely forty years of age. Oh.

But, I thought, nothing she said was making any sense to me. I couldn't place the balloons, or the light-blue turquoise color, or the patch of red on a large balloon, or a picture frame.

My mind was spinning frantically to make a connection to something, anything, but it could not.

Then the reading was over, and the magical twenty-dollar bill was wasted. *What a gyp,* I thought in great disappointment and left Janet's table with a mumbled, obligatory, "Thank you."

I was feeling so dazed and clouded, I wanted nothing more than to go home and put the day behind me.

The next day, when I was at the kitchen sink washing the morning dishes, with my mind relaxed, I gazed out the window, but the mixing bowl in my hand got my attention. I was turning it over in the warm, sudsy water to scrub, this treasured piece I had always used for baking because it was my grandmother's bowl.

Then a realization flooded my senses. *This* bowl! *Turquoise-blue,* the design on the side: many different old-time flying contraptions *and* hot-air balloons!

I could not believe it! I pulled the bowl out of the sink and held it to me, letting it soak my shirt. This precious bowl held pictures I hadn't really noticed in a very long time, and I began to sob in gratitude of the gift I had been given—*Proof!* My dad *was* with me there in my kitchen *and* he was with me that day with Janet, the clairvoyant. Now I understood—*he was here, and he had been playing tricks on me*—like he used to when I was a kid, to get my attention.

I took the turquoise bowl into the privacy of my home office, closed the door and I sat at my desk trying to process all of this— letting go of forty years of wonder and doubt.

My dad *had* stayed close to me. I looked up at the ceiling in acknowledgment of him, even hoping to *see* him, and asked softly, "Dad, are you here, now?"

In the act of looking up, I caught a glimpse of the framed award on the wall over my desk, where I sit every day, an achievement award, a graphic metal cut-out of a hot-air balloon and one part of the balloon was striped in red, just as Janet had said.

Duh! I work as a real-estate agent for ReMax *and* the logo IS a hot-air balloon.

During the reading, I was *hearing* the opposite of what I had *expected* to hear, and I had closed my mind. Now, relaxed and at home, I got it. My dad was doing his best to get my attention, to tell me he was proud of me and my achievements, by showing me the framed award plaques that have always been right here, above my head!

The blue kitchen bowl showed me he *is* near, and still the same dad who had played tricks on me.

Through the eyes of a woman with an extraordinary gift, I now had proof. Janet had not known me or had any information about me before I sat at her table, but she conveyed what my dad had been trying to tell me.

This experience taught me to keep my mind open in the belief that our loved ones do *not* die, they just move on to another side of life. And sometimes, our loved ones take a glimpse of how *we* are, and what we are doing, and are watching over us with love and pride.

This proof dispelled any doubt that lingered within me, I was completely certain that there *is* another side of life after leaving this one, a place from which our loved ones who have passed on can still see us, interact and talk with us, if we pay attention.

~ ~ ~

Just Because You Can't See Me...

At sixty-three-years of age, it was really fun to see myself as a teenager again, so full of life and questions. This opportunity came wrapped within a dream-experience, a chance to see myself, and exactly who I was, in my youth.

I had a vivid view of myself as I stood outside of me, having the point of view and mind of myself now.

I was seventeen and it had been a year since l lost my beloved father. I was in my own backyard with a gathering of my friends from the days of way back then. We were hooting and hollering and having teenage fun, and enjoying being out together after dark. The faces of these friends were so clear, though some had not crossed my mind since graduating high school so many years ago. But they were all gathered together now, right in front of me, on this warm summer evening as we played under the stars.

One of the boys had proudly brought a telescope he had just received. It was a good trade for a day's worth of yard work. He had accepted the trade, knowing that it needed some work and a few new parts, and he carefully left it in our front yard while we all partied in the back.

Sometime during the evening, in the dream, my father came outside, yes the one who had passed last year. There he was just as real and handsome as I remembered him. For whatever reason, he had decided to surprise us all and work on the telescope while we enjoyed ourselves.

Late into the evening, we began to wind down our party and walked out to the front yard to say our goodnights and were surprised to see my dad working on the telescope. No one was more surprised than me and I ran to hug the father I had missed so much. My friend though, seemed a little miffed, saying to my dad that he already knew it needed a *"Collimator Alignment"* my father added, "also a *'Poncet Platform Support'.*" Then my friend began to smile as they had now found common ground in telescope language.

"Dad, is it working now?" I asked, standing behind it, and squinting one eye as I looked through. But I could not *see* my father who was standing in front of it.

Frustrated that I couldn't see him, I took a step back and noticed a box nearby that contained many different optical lenses, all strung together. I tried to hold them up individually so I could look through them, and carefully rotated each glass lens, but that didn't work either. I couldn't *see* my dad through any of the lenses and, with each failed attempt, I lowered the lens and checked to make sure he was still there, that he had not left me, and that indeed, he was still there in front of me.

I repeated this several times, until he laughed and said, *"See, just because you can no longer see me, doesn't mean I am not here."*

I woke up with this message, but also with the strange telescope words, so different from my vocabulary. I knew that if I didn't write them down I would forget them, so I captured it all in my bedside journal.

Later that morning, I Googled "telescope parts" and sure enough, the words are actually there. The collimator is a part to "aide in the aligning of optical lenses in a telescope," and the poncet mount or stabilizer is there "to match the angle of the celestial equator." I could not believe my eyes. How wonderful to know the words given to me by my father, a man who had known nothing of fixing telescopes and had passed away long before owning them was commonplace. In 1969, few had the privilege of even looking through a civilian telescope; household computers and even simple calculators were nonexistent.

In this dream, my father had given me what is called "Evidential Proof," a way to more than feel or hope that he had really been with me in my dream; he had left me actual proof that it was so. He was with me and came to teach me a valuable lesson from the Other Side.

He also gave me a beautiful message; that he is *here,* even though *I* cannot see him and that:

> *Your loved ones are near you as well,*
> *Even though you cannot see them.*

~ ~ ~

Not Gone, Just Not Here

I was stopped at a red light the other day, on my way home from a hospice unit in Colorado Springs. I enjoy my service there, but tonight I was exhausted. I was too tired to cook, so I pulled off the freeway to pick up some takeout. Parked at the red light was my first opportunity to take a deep breath and, out the corner of my eye, I saw it.

'Amanda's Fonda', a familiar restaurant was now opening a new location, this restaurant that had meant something to me and to so many of us in Colorado Springs. Amanda had been a good friend, and the whole town in general was still dealing with the loss of her.

I missed her "momma make it better" way. She was a good ear to share troubles with, always resulting in a hug that just made you feel better. She had earned the reputation for taking in strays, people strays, lonely or displaced from family. She was a true friend—her home, her restaurant, all—giving solace. She had a "No One Left Behind" policy, all were invited, and her kindness gave the air an ease to just be you around her.

She was the official Momma to our biker crowd, the educated and hard-working bikers who spent their weekends polishing chrome and getting out their black leather for a day trip somewhere under the Colorado sun. The end of the ride would find us on a canyon road in Manitou Springs, We rode through the tree lined streets with the clouds directly over our heads, and would make our way to Amanda's restaurant for food and drinks. The parking lot would be full of well-heeled motorcycles, rows and rows of varying styles of Harleys, and a representation of a few other brands.

Long tables were set up and the staff would greet the group of us, Amanda, and her husband, owners, and a few of their closest friends. Our home away from home was their restaurant located creek side, and the large patio under the trees was soon filled with the lot of us, and our cold beers. It was Amanda's Fonda, and they willingly shared it with us all.

All of us loved Amanda, she told it like it was, but with an added soft pinch or a gentle slug in the arm. Her laugh was big and loud, and could be heard above all others, even in a crowded room. You always knew when Amanda was around.

She invented my husband Chris's favorite line, and used it often after listening to stories of his misdeeds. She would break out in laughter, saying, "You're so stuupppid!" and all of us would break out in laughter, including Chris. Inevitably, at some time in the evening, she would find a place to insert her sing-songy line, "No one *can* like a Mexi-*can*." She was proud of her heritage and her authentic food.

I could go on and on about Amanda, as it is an impossible task trying to capture the sum of her, the sound of her laughter, the love that oozed from within her, it was palpable and enduring as she looked in your direction with her candy-apple-red lipstick smile.

Amanda was lost to us way too soon, and no one better fit the statement that "only the good die young." Sadly, our group's rides became infrequent, as we had lost the glue of her and the joy of her. Momma was gone and the family began to fall apart.

I make a point of toasting Amanda, when I'm among those of us who remained friends. I never want to forget the example of the love and acceptance that she embodied.

And now as I sat at this red light and I see her name in lights, a second location created after her passing and the subsequent sale of the original creek-side location, I felt an instant sadness. How quickly life can change. I said aloud, "Oh, Manda, a new restaurant, it's you, but it's not you." I took a breath as I finished my thought, "I really miss you."

It startled me that I received a reply. I mean I could actually hear her loud happy voice as she piped in with a big, "HI!" followed by "Now, honey, don't feel bad. I'm OK. And guess what, I'M SKINNY NOW!!!"

Her words made me giggle. She was always so concerned about her weight. I heard myself giggle and thought, *Wait... what? Did I just really hear her?*

The light changed and it seemed the connection with Manda was gone. I drove home replaying the familiar sound of her unmistakable voice and laughter in my head. It had to be real. I mean—it was so real!

I will add here that this occurred in the early stages of my audible cognition and, apparently, Amanda was helping me understand and accept the gift—because I also heard from her the following day.

I was pulling warm clothes from the dryer and folding before wrinkles set in, my mind on nothing else but the drifting of mindless thoughts, when I heard, *"mija, mija."* (meehaw).

"Amanda?" I wondered out loud.

"Yes, it's me."

"Amanda, how are you?"

"I'm good, honey. I'm just checking in on you."

It felt so good to hear her call me honey again. I felt her love and care flooding over me, and I felt safe to ask her, "Amanda, there is a lot of spiritual stuff going on with me right now. Do you know?"

"Yes, I know, and I'm proud of you. You're doing good. Keep it up."

With that, she was gone. I was left wondering about the word *mija*. I had never heard her call me this before. Was it some kind of Spanish endearment?

A few hours later, my husband Chris came into my office to invite me to lunch. He had been thinking that we should try out the new Amanda's Fonda.

Okay, can the word *synchronicity* be inserted here—because I about fell off my chair! I had kept my conversations with Amanda to myself for now. But as we drove to the restaurant, all of it kept scrolling through my mind. Perhaps this was an opportunity to share my rising gifts of hearing from and talking to the dead.

This was not an easy subject to bring up, but Chris and I sat in the parking lot before going inside and I told him about my visits from our mutual friend. I was relieved that he did not shut me down. In fact, he suggested that we ask someone inside if they spoke Spanish and could they tell us the meaning of *mija*.

Our waiter did not speak Spanish but he brought one of the kitchen staff to our table. He said the meaning of *mija* is daughter.

Ahh, another piece of the mystery puzzle locked into place. Amanda had two daughters and, since her death, we hadn't seen much of either of them. The older was married with a young child; the youngest was now in her teens, living with her dad. Sadly, our connection to Amanda's husband wasn't as tight as it had been; he was trying to move on with his life and dating, as he should, and we were happy for him; but it was also hard to see him with anyone new, because Amanda's love for him and his for her had been so very deep. It was just weird watching him fall in love him with anyone else.

We knew that the sale of Amanda's restaurant had been a cause of family strife between little Amanda and her stepfather. When I later called him to ask about her, he told me there had been no communication between them in a number of years. He told us where he thought she worked now, and I knew that I had to see her.

Chris asked me, "Why doesn't Amanda just say to you, 'Hey, go see little Amanda for me, will you?'"

I explained, "That isn't how it works. Executing our free will is our greatest gift and it isn't their place to tell us anything or ask us to do anything for them." Then I added that I understood her nudge, and with a sly smile told him, "She used a name I didn't know, in a language I didn't understand, to prove that it is really her. This proof is an important step in my spiritual progression and acceptance of my gift, and now I am free to investigate it further if I choose. "

"Good point," he said. "That makes sense."

As we left the restaurant I thought, *Little Amanda, I am going to find you and deliver a message from your mom.*

It was a couple of days until Little Amanda was back on shift at her work in a busy downtown bar. It was a Sunday afternoon and the bar was slow. She seemed really glad to see me, telling me this was bringing up many memories of her mother.

"You are the spitting image of her."

"Yes, I've heard this many times before."

We spoke in broken moments between customers ordering rounds, small talk and memories. We talked of our mutual love for her mother and how we both missed her.

I was waiting for the right time to speak of Amanda's visits with me, a heavy topic. When I finally did, I found she was open to it and thankful to know that her mother was trying to communicate with her.

In hearing her mother's words mentioning her daughters, little Amanda told me, "I haven't really spoken to my little sister Alexis in a while, in the pains of growing up, she was always fighting with her father, eventually moving in with me," adding "but it didn't end well." She looked up at me as she reached for the right words. "My little sister has a strong will and would not mind me, either. She left mad at me, too. It has now been a couple of years since we've been in touch."

This was sad news. I pondered the severity of this as Little Amanda excused herself to assist other customers.

I sat waiting to finish our conversation and say our goodbyes, feeling that the message had been delivered. But as I waited, the door opened and a young woman came in and sat at the other side of the bar. It had been a few years since I had last seen her, but I was almost positive it was Alexis, the younger sister.

How could this be? I looked at her and tried not to stare. Little Amanda was working and I wasn't sure if she noticed her; but when she came back in my direction, I whispered, "Is that Alexis?"

"Yup," she answered quietly. "I have no idea why she is suddenly here today and seated at my bar. I haven't heard of her or spoken to her in a least a-year-and-a-half now."

Little Amanda kept serving customers and ignored her little sister. I picked up my drink and approached Alexis, because this coincidence was just stranger than fiction. I gave her a hug as soon as I made sure she remembered who I was, and we began talking of her mother.

"I miss her so much," she said. "My life is a bit disheveled now." She held back tears. "I don't know what to do, I'm nineteen *and* pregnant. I haven't even told my father about it yet. I'm here now as a sad little sister trying to make amends."

Mija, mija—the daughters—they needed each other now. From the Other Side, their mother was aware of the distance between them that needed to be shored up. I smiled, recognizing that so many pieces had fallen into place. Amanda had worked very hard on the perfect timing of this "coincidental" meeting, bringing all of us together at the same time. Hmmm....Dare I add that there are no coincidences, at least not of this magnitude?

I appreciate that there was a lesson in all of this for me too. A message from a dear friend, showing me to trust what I receive, that it is a gift and the messages can be very important.

I pray that these two will soften their hearts for each other and help each other. I know they both appreciated the message of their mother's watchful eye, even from the Other Side.

In the coined phrase of Rich Martini, they are "Not gone, just not here." and Amanda knew of the troubled waters below.

Having now delivered their mother's message, I left them both with hugs and the free will to do with this new information as they pleased. As I drove back home, I thanked Amanda *for showing all of us the way,* then had to chuckle at the cleaver orchestration of coincidences that brought us back together again, "Amanda, you haven't changed a bit, and I will love and miss you always."

~ ~ ~

Like a Dandelion in the Wind

There are people who cross your path in life and, when introduced, you can almost hear a "click" as if another piece of your life's puzzle has been set into place.

This is how I came to know Heather, a young girl in beauty school. She was working as an intern in an on the job-training program in the salon where I had been going for years.

"Hi, I'm Heather!" she said, beaming with a huge confident smile and a personality that just bubbled out of her little body, a breath of fresh air and an intoxicatingly free spirit. She was unafraid to tell it like it is and, when she would add a darling or a babe at the end of her styling suggestions, I began to trust her sense of style and fell in love with her FUNness immediately, paying no attention to the many years between our ages. We have shared stories of our lives and secrets in that styling chair, and over years together, have come to know of each other's spiritual beliefs as well. We shared books and stories and articles of what lies beyond this physical Earth. Where does one go *after?* was always a topic we ran with while waiting for my hair to dry.

Our strong foundation came in handy as life put us to the test, me in the loss my beloved sister, and now Heather has just learned that the cancer her mother has been valiantly battling is taking over and there isn't much time left for them together here.

One will set intent to remember the words of advice and love given by a loved one in their final days, and Heather spoke of a beautiful message her mother had given her in recognition of Heather's special gifts for the world, understanding who she was, and what she was meant to do in her life.

Heather's mother was wise, leaving her with an analogy of the dandelion, so fun to pick up that feathery white globe, bring it to your lips and blow, all of the ripe seeds spreading themselves by being carried in the breeze, to be deposited wherever the wind would take them.

This message created is a perfect reflection of Heather and her gifts and talents, a gift from her loving mother, an image and something tangible to hold on to.

It had only been only a few short months since her mother's passing, but as Heather would say, life goes on.

My hair really did need attention. My appointment was in a few days and I had not seen Heather since her mother's passing. I wanted to bring her a gift, something of meaning.

I tried desperately to find a flower, a replica of a dandelion, that Heather could keep at her workstation. I spent days going from store to store, but I could not find just the right thing and I was feeling a bit defeated as I got ready for my appointment that morning. I actually said aloud to Heather's mother, "Sorry, Cindy, I tried." I really had felt the need to give Heather the symbol of the dandelion. In the last few moments before leaving, when I turned on the computer to check for emails, my Facebook page was open and there it was: A picture of that wispy ball of a white dandelion with a multiplicity of seeds, poised and ready to dance through the air! Someone had decided to post this particular picture and sentiment at that same moment I was voicing my despair to her mother Cindy, and the words written next to the picture said it all perfectly:

A weed is a plant that has mastered every survival skill—except for learning how to grow in rows—be a weed.

I could not believe my eyes! This phrase was so perfectly Heather *and* her mother's message! I knew that Cindy had heard me and had come through with a special message for her daughter.

The messages are there, if we ask for them and pay attention. Our loved ones who are no longer with us in the physical sense are so happy to help us and give us what we need. They are near, they are listening, and they love us always. They are close, always close as we stumble along, encouraging us to be like a weed, to stop trying to grow in a row and to just be. Most importantly: to be like a dandelion, and to dance freely in the wind.

~~~

NOW

Yesterday was my sister Kaylyn's birthday. I sat on the edge of my bed, opened my journal and wrote down December 2. Sadly, this marked a year and six months since she passed away.

Then I wrote her a birthday note, starting with, "How much I Love and Miss you—You were always there for me." Next, I intended to write "*and I know you will always be there for me*", but I noticed I had actually written the word "*now.*"

I began to chide myself for messing up the letter. I would have to make a big scribble mark in the middle of my journal. I was just about to cross the word out when I stopped and really took a look at what I had written: "*You were always there for me...now.*"

I read it again. *Now.* I suddenly got it, the "aha" moment—Duh! She was with me *right now. She* had nudged me to write the word *now*, to show me she was with me *RIGHT NOW!*

I laughed out loud!

After reading this simple word over and over several times, I thanked her, telling her that I had *received her message, Loud and Clear.*

What could have been a melancholy day turned into something beautiful. It became a day for celebration. My sister had given me a gift on HER birthday, a special message to show me she was aware of what I was doing *and* she was here *NOW.*

I hold onto this message as an affirmation of our loved ones' continued awareness of those of us left behind—and if we are mindful and pay attention even to the smallest of signs, such as a misspoken three-letter word, we can remain in communication with them as well.

~ ~ ~

"Watching Over My Little Girl"

Last night, I had such a prophetic dream of Joan, my mother-in-law. She and I have been both friends and relations for more than twenty-four years, a relationship steadily built, and more than a mere mother/daughter-in-law relationship. We are truly friends. Over the years, we have shared many stories of our lives prior to knowing one another, sharing our hopes and dreams and the changes going on within us, deep meaningful stuff.

Now as I go through my spiritual awakening, experiencing and remembering wonderful gifts as they grow stronger, Joan listens to my stories and dream-experiences with love and appreciation for me. She shows sincere enthusiasm and without judgment of the content.

She has shared many of her own life experiences as well, of both happy times and true trials, beginning with the loss of her mother.

Joan was so very young—barely three years old—a vulnerable and motherless child when she was taken to spend most of her time to live with her caring grandmother and two aunts on a comfortable dirt farm. It was with the sincere intent to help her widowed father, a man whom she would later need protection from, protection that would never come. These were hard times, and it was never acknowledged that there was a desperate need to shield her from aggressive behaviors and sexual atrocities at the hands of her father.

It is hard to imagine all that is held so deep within Joan's soul. These were hard times indeed, and at a time when one did not speak of such depravities. Joan learned early on that she was to suffer in silence.

I wanted to do something special for her on Mother's Day. Her son and I came over, prepared to clean the porches and yard, haul away collected debris and power-wash her patio and outside areas. All of this work was offered with a loving intent to give her a nice fresh place to enjoy the summer outdoors. We even purchased new weatherproof chairs for her to relax in after finishing daily garden chores.

Before beginning the day's task, I stopped by the grocery store to pick up a few snacks for the long day ahead. I stopped short at the front of the store, mesmerized by the vast display of beautiful flowers set up for the enticement of an easy Mother's Day purchase. I just had to stop for a moment to smell the rows and rows of potted and hanging plants surrounding me. I had no intention of buying, as I had already purchased the gifts I had intended to give. I was only enjoying the sweet smells of the many varieties displayed.

I was pulling myself away when I spotted a pot full of the smallest lavender-colored flowers, it was just bursting with such a brilliant purple color, the blossoms spilling over the sides of the pot. It was especially pretty and, as I looked at it, I heard, *"Please give this one to my little girl!"*

In times past, I would have wondered, did I really just hear that? But I no longer question what I hear, and a knowing eased through me as I realized that I had just heard Joan's mother speaking to me ... and I didn't hesitate to do as she asked.

I picked up the plant and put it in my cart. Later, I tried to explain all of this to Chris and why I had come home with more than expected from the store, but he just shrugged as he often does about the "weird" things happening to me lately.

The day progressed, and we cleaned and worked as planned, and it was afternoon before we all took a seat in the new chairs. Joan was so very thankful for the day we had spent together and was expressing her gratitude when I told her, "I have one more surprise."

I went to the car to retrieve the pot of purple flowers. Joan has a love of flowers, too. As I carried them, her eyes watched the purple petals bounce and dance with a big smile on her face. "They're beautiful, Claudia!"

I agreed and with a smile said, "But they aren't really from me. They are a special gift..." I went on to reveal the details of why I had bought them."...and your mother so clearly asked me to *'please give these to my little girl.'* "

As we stood together Joan grasped the sentiment, and that the flowers were truly from her mother. Her eyes filled with tears, she said, "I haven't been anyone's little girl in a very long time... I was forced to grow up very fast." She moved quickly from the circumstances of the three-year-old motherless child. "I've spent most of my life in a primal mode of pure survival." She smiled bittersweetly. "I couldn't give in to remembering, or even letting myself really experience, a time when I had ever been anybody's little girl."

It was a beautiful moment to be a part of, as this stunning realization poured through her. She was allowing herself to feel her mother's love and the fact that she was really near her and had been watching over her for all of these eighty-plus years; that she still loved her little girl, this little girl standing next to me, with all of her heart.

I was in gratitude for playing a part in such a beautiful moment on Mother's Day, and a few nights later I had this vivid dream:

Chris and I were attending a show starring many healthy and spry senior citizens from the community. We were enjoying watching Joan and the other ladies on stage in a full costumed dance routine, when all quickly changed as it does in dreams and the stage morphed into an outdoors scene and suddenly we were all dressed in winter attire.

We watched as Joan and the ladies began to sing together, now on skis. Each member of this singing group would take a turn to wave goodbye, signaling the finale of the show as they skied off into the distance. Joan was toward the back of the pack of skiing ladies and, as they crossed a gated opening, one of the ladies near Joan began to fall, causing Joan to spill onto the hard snowy ground as well. The crowd took a collective breath.

Chris and I began to run in the snow toward her, but as we got closer to her, she suddenly turned into a little girl. She was now a three-year-old little girl wearing a "Shirley Temple" kind of dress, cute in her white ankle stockings and red-buckled shoes. I took note of her soft brown hair, cut into an Asian style, the bangs chopped very short, the rest combed straight and cut just above her ears.

Tears streamed down her face as she ran toward us, and she held out her arms for me to lift her up. I scooped her up to me, and she buried her little face into my chest.

What came next was a realization of all that my mother-in-law was, who she really was and had ever been. In that exact moment of holding her, I felt all of the caretakers she had ever had as a child move through me—her mother, her aunts, her grandmother. They were all there, all together, holding this little one, this vulnerable child and all her hurts. All of us were working together, comforting her whimpers and tears.

She clung to me, but I was only one of the many there in that hug. I promised her, "All will be alright, and to the best of *our* ability, we will make it all okay."

I write this, wrapped in a sweater on the first real cold day of the coming winter—but I am feeling a warm breath against my cheek, the softest of a touch, so quiet and reverent, and I know it is the touch of Joan's mother. She is here to help me tell this story, because she wants us to know, she will always love and be near her little girl and will continue to try to make it all okay.

~ ~ ~

I'm the Crack, Mom

I am getting better at connecting to the Other Side since my sister Kaylyn's passing. I have put the grief of her loss into a positive practice. I have worked toward establishing a connection and have felt her eagerness to help me. That is my sister's true personality, and I know she has graciously stayed near and available to assist me in developing this gift of communication. I am grateful that her patience with me has never wavered as I continue to learn.

I was visiting our mother, who was still living in the same house, the one we grew up in, purchased in 1958, a brick rambler three bedroom, one bath.

As I stood in front of the bathroom mirror with the door ajar, allowing the steam from the shower to escape while I blow-dried my hair, I glanced out into the hallway which held a wall full of framed family photos, a proud display of growing children, grandchildren and great-grandchildren, forever frozen in time. One display in particular caught my attention, a collage of various photos of my sister in her young growing years.

As I stood there combing my hair, I reflected on Kaylyn's life, and now my life without her in it. My mind was wandering under the roar of the dryer in my ears, and it must have created the perfect storm, because I *heard* her! I could hear Kaylyn on my left side, not really in my ear but in my head. It wasn't my voice, it wasn't my thoughts, it was *her* voice *in* my thoughts and it was plain as day.

"What you looking at?" she asked in a playful tone.

I was so excited to hear her voice I replied without hesitation. "Kaylyn, is that you?" I already knew it was so I continued, "I'm looking at your pictures. You are so pretty."

"Yeah, well I'm prettier now," she retorted and we both giggled, like sisters do.

Then I became a little sullen. "I miss you, Kay"

"I know you do. I miss you, too. But I'm here, right? Please tell everyone. I'm here always."

"I will, Kay."

"Keep working on Mom, okay," she added. *"She needs to know this."*

"I am. Believe me, I am. I love you, Kay."

And before I could no longer hear her, she told me, *"I love you, too."*

Going about the business of the day, I finished drying my hair; but the love and gratitude I felt for this new ability to hear from my angel sister from time to time was so elating I couldn't hold in the joy of it all. It was so very wonderful!

How could I share this miracle without people thinking I was desperately making it up, or nuts?

Then my joy spilled into tears, because *I knew I had to share this with our Mom,* though I wasn't exactly sure how to start. I sat her down and relayed Kaylyn's message. I thought she would be elated too, but instead she focused only on her own question. "How come you are getting all of this?"

I thought a moment. "Mom, I am no more special, nor do I have any better abilities, than anyone else. I just...listen. I am open to hearing and feeling them. Perhaps it is because I believe so strongly that it is possible, that it makes it possible.

"Imagine," I said to her, "*wanting* to communicate with those left behind—Kaylyn was gone from us so very quickly with a brain aneurysm—Mom, she was here experiencing a normal day, and then in one swift moment, she was gone. There was no opportunity for final hugs and goodbyes. Can you imagine her frustration?

"And what about all of the others with her, anxious to let their loved ones know they are alright too, that they are near them and love them always. Now imagine they would really like to tell us these things, but they don't speak the same way as they did before. They no longer have the heavy body they were used to, and speaking and listening is on a whole new level. They are light and free now, and they use a kind of thought instead of verbal speech, so we can't hear them with our earthly ears.

"Mom, imagine how excited you would be to find someone here, still on this earthly plane who was really trying to listen and understand, someone who was open-minded about being able to hear them, even opened just a crack, believing it is possible to listen and hear them—and actually talk back to them and relay their messages.

"Wouldn't it be a relief and joy for them to know they have been heard, that they can say what was left unsaid, and their "*I Love You's*" can still be heard and shared."

I paused for a moment and laughed out loud. I had the perfect analogy. "Mom, *I'm* the crack!" I pointed to the top of my head. "I'm the crack in the veil." I grinned, and she did too, I had 'cracked through' the ice between us, and given her an explanation she seemed satisfied with.

Now, I am playfully using this visual analogy for those who don't understand how this connection can be.

The *crack* is a visible divide that can be seen or felt from the Other Side, and I am working hard to enhance it on my end, possibly turning my crack into a canyon someday. I am working hard to be a bridge between two worlds. I will continue to be open and listen and will definitely share what I hear.

~ ~ ~

They're Putting Their Coats On, Mom. They're Coming.

After more than two weeks in the Intensive Care Unit, my mother was frustrated at her lack of ability to bounce back. She knew she wasn't getting any better and was exhausted living in a suspended state of *"Do you want the good news or the bad news?"* because she remained no better and no worse.

Though she never questioned the reasons why, I knew she was growing weary and bored. She was tired of lying around *cognizant* of every breath and the toll it was taking to draw and expel each one.

The night before she passed, I dreamed of her large childhood family. She was one of nine brothers and sisters, all had passed long before her, and I saw them all in my dream.

It was as if it were filmed in the days of the first home movies, a grainy black-and-white film. It began as the camera scanned a grand ballroom. Within moments, the attention was focused on her siblings. Her brothers were getting ready for a party and were dressed in their finery, addressing button down shirts. Her sisters and sisters- in-law were in their best dresses; some wore netted hats, all were garnished with large pieces of costume jewelry, and a large flowered corsage was pinned to each dress. My aunt Bev has been gone for so very long now, but I instantly recognized her—stylishly wrapped in a mink stole, as she was always dressed to the nines. Her brothers pulled on topcoats over their suits and reached for their hats.

I watched as they all began to gather, and I recognized each and every one, favorite aunts and uncles forming top and bottom rows, taking time to pose for a family picture—or perhaps creating a special moment for me to get a really good look at them all.

I knew instantly why they were dressing up and putting on their coats. It was finally time to bring the last one of them home. A grand reunion was being prepared in this Great Hall and my mother would no longer be the little sister left behind. They were all to be reunited at last.

When my mother woke that morning in her hospital bed, she was the same, no better or worse than the day before. The few people I told that she was leaving today wondered about my sanity, but I have learned there is no reason to doubt what I see.

As the day wore on and Mom and I knew we were facing the inevitable, I shared the dream with her. She was so happy to know this, and it gave her peace as she entered the last phase with calm repose. They were coming to get her.

By four that afternoon, my mother was with them all again. My tears were mixed with happiness for her. She had earned this. Her contract was complete and it was time now for the grandest of celebrations, in the grandest of halls.

~ ~ ~

11

Patience Is Another Virtue

~~ ~ ~~

Be as the tree

I am always searching for more knowledge of the Hereafter. I read and research books, and I have talked with many who have a firsthand knowledge of it themselves, through a near-death experience.

I have been graced in the last few years with many of my own firsthand experiences, receiving messages from the Other Side. The communications I have received are real, and there is no more room for doubt, as my experiences are backed up with evidence that I now no longer require but always enjoy.

When I am immersed in the ordinary ebb and flow of life, and the doubts begin to arise, it is because it can sometimes be days or even weeks without my hearing anything. Those times can become very trying, and it can become overwhelmingly lonely when spiritual messages are paused.

One morning, I was experiencing this familiar ache of loneliness. After praying, I asked aloud, "Hey, where is everyone? Spirit guides, Heavenly Father, Kaylyn, where are you? This spring you were so close, but now I don't feel you anymore. I miss you and I am feeling so very alone."

It was but a few moments later that I heard, *"Look out your window"*, as a fluid wave of words flowed into my mind. I scrambled for pen and paper to capture them:

Be As the Tree

Be as the tree.
Stand tall, reaching ever upward, towards the light.
Yet stay grounded in the earth, accepting what is given in
sun and rain and snow.
Drink of knowledge to quench the thirst,
but mindful of staying grounded in the present.
Take on only what can be held in NOW.

Seasons will bring change to the look and shape of the tree.
Expect and accept these changes, at times full and bursting
forth with color, then dormant, waiting for another
chance at fulfilling its destiny, as leaves and fruits come
forth to be shared.
Let your branches bend with the breeze,
but anchor roots sturdy against the winds.
Experience patience and quiet, and ready yourself for the
next cycle of growth.

Experience all in your days.
Give your shade and shelter, your fruit and beauty, to those
around you, then rest and let the quiet voice surround
you.

Now as you cry and your branches lay barren, know that I
will always be with you. You are not alone. You are
never alone.
It is all as it should be.

This unexpected moment of grace calmed my angst and worry, and reminded me, *"All is as it should be,"* in Zen-like simplicity, *"Be as the tree."*

~ ~ ~

Of Being Bullied and Left Out

Last night, I had a dream-experience of being in a school classroom. I was a preteen girl who, for some reason, had been targeted by her teacher.

The teacher had decided not to include me in her lessons and had me standing in the back of the classroom all day. I was never given books or materials to work with, and she never even addressed me.

The other students didn't understand her behavior toward me either, but they were wrapped up in their own schoolwork. Although they did play with me at recess and I was sincerely liked by them, the classroom was different. It was everyone for themselves, and I was alone, excluded from every opportunity the others were given.

There was to be a graduation program and all of the students were on stage, singing and reciting memorized lines. I was excluded from this performance also, left to sit alone in the auditorium and watch all the others.

Two men entered the auditorium just as the real program started. They chose chairs near me. I smiled politely at them as they sat down. Within moments, they asked me why I wasn't part of the group on stage. I explained, to the best of my limited understanding, why this was happening, then offered to bring them each a glass of water, inquiring about their comfort, if they were too warm, could I put away their coats? I didn't know it but they were there to watch the performance and to pick out an exceptional student who would be given further training, which would lead to a great job in the future.

At the end of the program, the gentlemen who had been studying all of the children were asked by the teacher, "Which student have you chosen for your honored position?" She proudly held out her arm toward the stage of students.

Both men stood and one said, "Yes, we have made a final decision of who will go further in our specialized program."

They both turned to me, and said, "We are both impressed by

your sweet demeanor and offer of service, and pleased that your mind has not yet been corrupted by the nonsensical rhetoric the others have been subjected to by the teacher."

The teacher stood dumbfounded, as everyone's attention focused on me...

With that, I woke up.

I lay there in the dark, feeling victorious, in a *Little House on the Prairie* Laura Ingles kind of way—but the pain of being excluded and not understanding why lingered on. I lay in my bed with an underlying and unreachable ache, the dream still carving its lessons into me. The teacher had done her job well, as I did *not* feel normal and like the others and knew that something about me had kept me from being able to blend in.

Was there something about me that was so noticeably different? I didn't understand what the teacher saw or didn't see in me that she saw in the others. Her treatment of me made me feel outside of and less than the others. It gnawed at my self-esteem and the soft, malleable parts of me, leaching into my bones, the very frame with which I stand, my legs and spine giving way, retracting, my back losing precious inches, shrinking, crouching, cowering. My heart, too, quivered—in the loss of itself, I wasn't even likable, how could I possibly love myself? I must not be worthy of love, and pity anyone who offers theirs to me, without understanding the great risk of loving me in my worthless state of being.

This is what the dream revealed to me, feelings that are new to me, but are feelings suffered by so many. I am grateful for this very real emotional experience—as I lie safely in my room. I cry for those who suffer this emptiness on a daily basis, I was given internal knowledge of the silent grief of a child who is bullied and left out, now an epidemic in this world.

I am grateful this dream had a happy ending and my bully got hers. Sadly, this is rarely the consequence. After my tears, I am able to ease back into the safe reality of my own life, but the experience of being the one bullied and left out, has not been pushed so far out of reach that it cannot be accessed, it has been engrained into me. I now pay more attention to others around me, especially children. I make a point of looking for the child who is not fitting in, who is not equipped to deal with this type of situation.

I pray that we will all pay more attention *and* will intervene whenever we see this happening to another—before a point is reached of no return, suicide or a body or mind stunted in growth, that it begins to turn inward and on itself, with all hope of love and acceptance pushed away.

We all want to conform to what is deemed normal. We want to fit in and be included, and sometimes this conformity comes hidden underneath a great deal of suffering. Perhaps somehow, someway, in a faraway land of non-conformance, there is a reward in store for those who remain unique, humble and kind.

~ ~ ~

~ ~ ~

The Gift of a Friend

The unknowing teachers along the path
Are the gifts of the ones I have called friend
The ones with whom I have entwined and shared time
In both longevity or brief encounter
They are nevertheless placed lovingly,
As bookmarks in my life
As I work through theory and insight
Rounding hard edges into palatable balls
To be swallowed whole
All of my friends are etched into my soul
Each a helper
A bringer of light in their own way

~ ~ ~

12

New Dresses
& Other Gifts

~ ~ ~

The Gift of Communication

I woke in the middle of the night, the room was dark, but I didn't need to see. I could feel the smile on my face, and my heart was beating a rhythm of pure joy.

I had dreamed of my father, long gone from this world but forever loved and missed. Also of my sister, who passed just a short time ago. But last night they were both in my dream-experience and I held onto myself as I began the recall of it, to memorize every last detail.

In the dream, my younger sister and I were children, seven and ten years old. It was the night before starting a new school year and we were excited to leave summer behind. We were trying on our chosen outfits for that important first-day impression, admiring our new shoes and socks and matching hair barrettes. All were double-checked, making sure everything was just right. Our new dresses were simple cotton, sewn by our mother. The world seemed perfect, and so were our dresses, and the full circle skirt was our enticement to twirl and spin and laugh together as we watched each other's dresses catch the air and become fluffy and full.

Our gleeful laughter and giggles caught our father's attention, and he danced with us as we circled about in our fashion show. He called us his "precious beautiful girls" as we twirled about. We loved being the center of his attention, smiling and watching us happily playing together, his precious beautiful girls. We were young and sweet, our lives happily balanced in our own perfect world, we were daddy's little girls.

The happy scene changed on a dime, just moments before we were all laughing together, and now he was gone, his exit so abrupt that his voice still echoed in our ears. *"Daddy's girls, precious girls."* Now our daddy was gone, and we were left to hold onto one another in our mutual grief and loss, knowing he was never coming back.

The echo of his voice began to fade and was becoming a part of the distant past as the scene changed again. We were still holding each other up but we have grown, we were now adults, still needing each other and still missing our dad. The scene deepened in a solemn richness and a kind of reverence overtook the air around us as we found ourselves in the middle of a spiritual ceremony, a form of unveiling in which we were receiving instructions and teachings, remembering what had been clouded from our memories about our purposes and paths.

We were being allowed to remember our spiritual gifts and talents. What was specifically said to my sister Kaylyn I cannot recall, but what was said to me I will never forget. I was told, "You have been given a special gift." As the words were spoken they became physical and lofted in the air where I could read them. I repeated them as they edged toward me and entered my mouth; I could *feel* the words—physical, solid words that had weight and density to them—and each one had a separate taste. I touched my lips as they entered into me—I was receiving the gift of "Speaking to the Dead." I was to use my mouth and my words to connect the Afterlife with this physical one, as a "Bridge of Communication."

Kay and I stood together in acceptance of what was being given to us. After the ceremony was over, Kay turned to me and in true sibling style said, "Whoa, I'm jealous, because if you can speak to the dead, that means you'll get to talk to Dad again soon!"

Happy at the thought of this ability, I started giggling, and I was pleased at getting to be first in a sisterly competition. Then, at the exact moment of this thought the scene changed again, and like blowing sand, Kaylyn was gone.

Standing alone, the air that took Kay away still wafting around me, I was left to accept the fact that she too was never coming back. I was now to hold onto myself. I folded into an acceptance of Kay's departure, and was struck with comical sisterly jealousy. I knew right then that she was with Dad, erasing the years between them, filling him in on all he had missed.

Skunked, I laughed out loud. My little sister had trumped me. She had won our loving competition of who would be first of us to talk to Dad again. I laughed at the game itself, happy for both of us—as I too would be able to speak with him again through this new awakened gift.

The dream was ending and a sign came into view, a large poster board, the edges laced with a fancy green border. It was displayed on an easel, like they do when watching a play. Such signs are usually notes for the audience like "Intermission" or "Applause", but this sign was different, because it was sent by my little sister:

Words From the Mouths of Sisters,
Can Create Funny Tales and Stories

I laughed out loud, then bowed and saluted her, giddy in her celebration of winning the sisterly competition.

I am left with sincere gratitude to have relived one of the many happy times I shared with my dearest younger sister Kay as we twirled and danced. And most especially, I am grateful for the opportunity to hear her voice and our father's again. The laughter we shared in this dream was from many years ago, yet only a moment ago. The memory is so sweet and so close that I can still reach out and touch it. It is still there when I close my eyes. I can see us, two beautiful dark-haired pixies dancing in the joy of our new dresses and in the love of a father that will never end.

The unexpected gift of the spiritual ceremony was bigger than my comprehension at the time, but I now have grown into an understanding and appreciation of this ability and purpose; and I am working on the use of it, finding that exercising the insights and contact is much like exercising a muscle, as either can wither with atrophy if not practiced. So, I work very hard to be a bridge of communication with the Other Side as it was offered to me, and humbly finding much value in its use.

My beloved little sister truly has been instrumental in my learning to use this gift and has communicated with me many times since her passing, each time with a sisterly love jab and giggle, adding another funny tale or story to share.

~ ~ ~

Hi, My Name Is Brad

Pueblo, Colorado is a small town some sixty miles from our home in Colorado Springs.

My husband Chris and I had driven there one afternoon for business, deciding to make it a special day by having dinner at Rosario's, an upscale authentic Italian restaurant near the city center.

We were able to pick our own table, as it was still early, no dinner rush yet. We wanted to take our time and enjoy a bottle of wine and watch the action of the river walk, our table sitting against the big window as spring's warm evening sun sent streams of light onto our red-checkered tablecloth.

We began to relax, talking and laughing, spending much needed time to enjoy each other. All felt right with the world. More wine? Yes, please! Ahh, feeling good," yes" both of us wearing a relaxed smile, as we looked over the menu.

As we decided what to order, we noticed a large group of people coming through the door, an entire family of grandparents, aunts, uncles and kids, and they were headed right toward us!

Chris and I both took a quick glance at the table next to us, set for this large party, tables pushed together with lots of plates, and both of our faces changed to OH NO! In our rush to nab the table in front of the beautiful picture window, we had neglected to notice the large group place setting next to us, and the waitress had not mentioned anything about the large group that would soon be joining us here.

We had our pick of preferred spots, now we were kind of stuck.

We sat helplessly watching as the family took their seats. One man about forty years of age was being very particular about his seat, checking all of them out on the other side of the table. Not yet satisfied, he began to come toward us, to the empty chair at the end of the table. He wore a tilted, red ball cap, and it was obvious he had intellectual disabilities. Before sitting, he looked over directly at me, with the biggest of smiles coming from under his funny old cap.

"Hi," he said proudly, "my name's Brad!"

By the tone and intention of his words, I could tell that he had spoken this line over a million times before. Then he stood there in silence, smiling and waiting for my reply.

"Hi, Brad. I'm Claudia." I said.

Then he reached across our table, extended his hand, reaching out for mine.

His enthusiasm for everything around him was boundless: for meeting someone new, for being out with his family, for life in general. I took note of all of it, though it began to feel a bit awkward as he continued to stand and stare at me just a little too long. I broke into the hanging moment saying, "Brad, this is my handsome husband Chris."

Brad put out his hand for Chris to shake, too. Then Brad's family noticed what could become an annoying situation and quickly hustled him into his seat.

Now sitting elbow to elbow with Brad, Chris looked at me with a silent, should we get out of here? But we both ended up shrugging our shoulders and picking up our wine glasses.

Brad was soon distracted from us by his family giving him a menu and asking what he wanted to eat for dinner. Chris and I attempted to continue our own conversation but were frequently interrupted by Brad's big toothy grin and continued introductions. "Hi! My name's Brad" over and over again. His family shushed him, to leave us be. His mother had a frustrated tone in her voice, apparently worn out by this familiar behavior.

At one point in my life, I would have moved to another table, on the other side of the restaurant, showed annoyance or at least ignored Brad—as Brad cut into our conversation every few minutes, "Hi, I'm Brad" or "What's your name?" or "You're my friend" or "You're nice."

Today, however, I found myself looking at his family dynamic, the tired and embarrassed mother, after forty years of shushing him. His younger brother, to whom he repeatedly said, "You're my friend" and his brother would reply, "I'm your best friend, Brad." The rest of the family was oblivious, as they stared into their menus.

This would have been a long miserable evening if both Chris and I had chosen to look at it that way. There are many times in life that we can *choose* how we look at and react to a situation. Tonight, we made a conscious decision to stay positive and continue to enjoy ourselves.

As the evening went on, I let myself be drawn into the energetic vibration and pure joy that Brad exuded. The atmosphere was full of it. He was sweet and full of life, no conflict or comprehension of life's hardships. He still carried the child-like innocence that we all start with but eventually lose as we grow and engage in the world. Brad had not lost his and I found myself looking past his demeanor and ventured deeper, I looked into his soul, and his choice to be here in this capacity, with this particular experience in the world. What lesson or test was he here for? Perhaps he was here as a perfect example or lesson for his family, and others, of patience, unconditional love and understanding. The gift of Brad.

The interruptions continued, but slowed over time, and I would be replaced as would Brad's new best friend by the waitress taking his order. His dinner came, and Chris and I were able to continue with our own evening. It wasn't until we stood to leave that Brad noticed us again and shot me the warmest of smiles. "That's my friend, Claudia!"

I was touched that he remembered my name and this time it was I who approached him. I took his hand in a love and appreciation of him. "Brad, you are a good man." This statement was an echo, something his brother had said to him several times throughout dinner. Then I added, "Thank you for being my friend." We shook hands and I started to turn to leave. He hollered out. "I'll call you when I get a phone!" We all giggled when he said that, the sentiment so sweet, not lost on any of us. I replied, "Okay, you call me then. Bye, Brad."

Chris and I finished the evening at the waterway, holding hands as we walked along the river walk, enjoying the beautiful transition of light, as the sun began to set. I was filled with the joy and love that Brad had brought into the dining hall. I thought about his spirit and who he really was—feeling he must be an advanced soul, doing this job here and now on this earth—a radiant beam of light and love for the whole world to feel.

Brad is playing his part in this the grand scheme of things, raising the frequency and vibration of the world. I felt myself feeling proud of him as he was doing his part, and also proud of my own behavior, and recognizing and appreciating the reasons why we need the Brads in this world.

I know I will think of Brad from time to time, the impression of him forever stamped onto my heart, his joy and love of all things is palpable, I felt honor for him in his job and how well he is doing it.

~ ~ ~

Ava's Magical Christmas Bowl

I've been told I'm hard to buy for, that I have such a particular taste. I'm sorry if this is true, because I do appreciate a thoughtful gift as much as anyone.

I have a fondness for what my children have deemed "pretties" or shiny objects made of stone or glass. I have a beautiful collection of pottery and vases, chimes and the like, so many gifted and put out for display. I get teased for the sheer volume of them throughout my home. With five children three step-children and nine grandchildren—counting birthdays, Mother's Days, and Christmas—I have racked up some really wonderful gifts.

I am greeted each morning with a choice of coffee mugs that hold the sweet faces of my grandchildren. I delight in holding a steaming cup as I relive special moments with them shown in the pictures printed on the mugs. One mug in particular is painted by hand, in brilliant orange and signed with a small purple handprint of my granddaughter Ava, a smooshed purple handprint that captures how little she was once. It is one of my favorite things, and I tell her often how much I love it.

This brings me to a scene in Ava's living room last night. It is now a couple of days after Christmas, and most of the presents that once resided under the tree have already been disbursed. But there was one that I could see Ava was especially excited about, not about the present she was receiving but the one she was giving. She held it out to me so carefully, her face so full of pride, offering it to me with both hands extended. Honestly, the look on her sweet face was present enough as she stood in front of me, anxiously waiting for me to open it, and in turn, looking for the reaction on my face.

I carefully unwrapped this beautiful, hand-painted ceramic rendering of many large leaves coming together in unison, to form the bowl. It was special. She was so quiet and sweet, as her mother explained the care Ava had put into her choice of the bowl's shape and design. The colors she had used were not from a giant display or happenstance. Rather, she had carefully thought out every color, with me in mind, and worked hard on a color-blending technique to make the bowl extra special and worthy of display among the other "pretties."

Ava will be nine years old next week, and not so easily fooled by the use of the word *magic*. I know when she hears that I call it a magical bowl, she will want an explanation of why. Maybe someday she will understand that the magic is in the way the bowl makes me feel every time I look at it, that there can be a physical expression of love given, especially when words are inadequate or fall off into the ether in the busy rhythms of our everyday life routines. But when I look at Ava's magical bowl, I marvel at the care and love she displayed in her gift to her grandmother, and I believe there is much magic in that.

~ ~ ~

Lovely Dreams and Other Presents

My mother came to me in a dream the other night. She looked so young and beautiful, the softest of light framing her face. Her hair was brown, the color of so many years ago, before the grays of age had taken hold. I basked in the warmth and sweetness of her smile, even more radiant than my happiest memories of her.

At her side was my stepfather Ray. Together, they looked very much like the young couple they had been in the early years of their marriage.

She began telling me that she and Ray wanted to bring me a gift, and Ray held out a large pouch made of dark-brown cloth, folded over into three flaps.

The first flap held two strange-looking metal headset devices.

On the first, I could see no visible plug-in holes or cords, and no soft rubber pieces to place into the ears. The headpiece was made from a heavy black metal and had two metal nubs protruding from the core. The intention of the nub was not to go into the ear but rather to be placed at the hollow spot behind the ears; the metal halo went from just below the shoulder, over the head, then back down to the opposite shoulder. The second object was similarly shaped but smaller, and the metal was a corroded color of brown.

Both looked like they came from a medieval museum. My mother said that wearing them would help me to "listen" because they were from someplace wonderful and they wanted to share it with me.

The idea of using these devices was so much like my stepfather, Raymond F. Jones. He had been a gifted science-fiction writer in the 1950s and 1960s. He had many credits to his name, including his most proclaimed book: *This Island Earth*, which was adapted into a film in 1955.

These devices just seemed to have his name all over them, inventions from the Other Side from a great inventive and scientific mind.

The second flap contained a shawl or wrap for my shoulders. It was of the softest of fabrics, a delicate weave; just touching the folded edge of it, within the flap, brought my fingertips an incredible comfort. I began to pull it out of the flap, pulling and pulling some more. The length seemed to grow longer and longer, like a magician's trick. It kept growing longer and longer, seemingly without end.

I began to wrap myself in it, turning around and around. Then my mother took the other end and began wrapping herself in it.

We delighted in this special dance together, winding, turning, wrapping and laughing, and we hugged and fell together when we reached the middle.

After these blissful moments of laughing together, she quieted herself and took my face in her hands and said, *"Remember this always. We are tied together, we will always be wrapped up in each other, and whenever you need comforting, put on this wrap and you will be able to feel me with you."*

Ray had stepped back during our dance, but my Mother stayed near as I opened the third and final flap on the pouch. *"This gift is from Ray,"* my mother said as I gazed upon seven stone necklaces with chains of gold, the length of the chains shorter than my usual style.

I knew my mom heard this thought because she acknowledged me with a smile and a little chuckle, and that I had yet to understand their special purpose. All of this was said in a telepathic exchange.

I took one of the polished stones into my hand and ran my fingers over it, noticing the smooth flat surface and the lightness of its weight. It was cut from something much larger, as if it had been sliced, to expose the exquisite colors and varieties of patterns. It reminded me of Mexican Lace Agate, but even more dramatic in the depth of its grains and color blends. It was like green tourmaline blended into a ruby red pattern that swirled into blue lapis, dotted with turquoise.

Some of the colored stones were translucent, some were opaque, and all were captured within this smooth slice. They were all beautiful in their individuality, one no more beautiful than the next. I look forward to the time I will learn about and use these necklaces for their intended purpose.

I do not remember saying goodbyes or even if I had the chance to thank Ray for the wonderful gifts: the headphones, the wrap, and the necklaces. The greatest gift was to see my mom and Ray again, young, happy and still good friends, still helping each other as they did in this life. I will forever hold onto this memory of laughing and dancing with my mother and our joy as we wrapped ourselves together, for the ability to comfort each other in the knowing that we will always be tied together.

~ ~ ~

~ ~ ~

She knows what makes me laugh
She knows what makes me cry
Tightly wound
Forever bound
My sister Kay and I

~ ~ ~

13

Of Sisters

~ ~ ~

Sisters on the Beach
A love letter to my sister

Dear Kaylyn,

I'm sitting in the sand on a beach in Half Moon Bay, just outside San Francisco, California. It's the day after Thanksgiving and I am reflecting on all I have to be thankful for, my family and children, good friends, sweet grandbabies, and my handsome husband who is settled into a chair next to mine.

With toes in the sand, I tilt my face toward the warmth of the sun and smile. It is a perfect day, indeed.

I'm watching the ocean as the waves break and roll along the sand. It is a sound as loud and booming as a jet engine. Yet, I find it peaceful. I love getting lost in its roar.

There are few others on the beach with us, and my attention to the waves is interrupted as I notice two women walking in the sand, their heads poised together, deep in conversation with one another and completely oblivious to anyone else around them. They are entirely "with each other." The closeness of their bodies suggests a familiarity, not romantic but of sisters. I search for the likeness in their faces, and find it. Yes, sisters.

I cannot help the instantaneous tears I shed now over the physical loss of you as I watch them, bumping shoulders, arms and hands as they walk together. There's no "Oh, sorry" or "Excuse me." Not with sisters. The bumping and brushing up against one another isn't even noticed. It is an accepted closeness born of years of sharing rooms, beds, toys and clothes; and the like of this closeness was something we squandered until almost too late.

I am so grateful we woke up in time and chose to be together in the last few years of your life. The ache of the loss of you remains, and I do not attempt to hold back my grief when it arrives suddenly. It is mine, and I own it. I do not look to share it. It's my own to feel, and I am grateful for it. This is a world of dualities and parallels, and I feel sadness and loss because I loved, and I am okay with that.

You, my dear sister, will always be in my heart and my soul. We are connected into infinity as guardians of one another. And I feel your assistance as I open spiritual doors. I feel your gentle pushes and your soft whispers. I know the feel of you, as you are still close, and I feel the bumps into one another when I pay attention and allow myself to feel you there. I can hear you when you talk to me, and I know with certainty that you hear me when I talk to you.

I want to thank you in this time of Thanksgiving for all you continue to do for me, and for the closeness we share now. In many ways, we are closer than ever before.

Thank you for the sisterly nudges towards the doors of enlightenment that I know are mine alone to open. Somehow, I feel this was part of our contract together, for you to go first and nudge your older sister along the path. I was always the free spirit, enjoying the freedom of my emotions, unafraid to show and use them with abandonment—while you held back in envy, disliking even a hint of the loss of control. You grew up even-keeled with a touch of temperance, while I drifted between bouts of happy to sad, and tears to laughter, which I own, too. I also know that you can now appreciate me and my hardheaded emotional ways.

You smile at me now with a heavenly grin, and I feel you take my hand with a sisterly familiarity into knowing, because you are sharing what you are learning from the Other Side with me, while I am still here, caught up in the humanness of earth.

Now you flit about in enlightened energy. You tickle my cheek and blow in my ear, especially when I need to smile. I feel you, Kay, and my heart is full, and all is O-Kay... As long as I can cry openly when I miss the physical of you and for the want of that sisterly unapologetic bump of a shoulder from time to time.

I love you, little Sister of mine—you are the only one I will ever have. I now hold the word Sister in a kind of reverence. I enjoy saying it, hearing the reverberating sound of it, and reveling in the emotion of what it means to me.

I write this letter to you, intending to share it openly, in its full emotional splendor. My hope is that the expression of loss will be of benefit to all sisters who can still make time to walk and talk together in an intimate sharing of putting their heads together, on a beach, or a trail, or down a city street. I will appreciate watching the gentle dance in their body language and recognizing that, yes—they are sisters—and it will make me smile even through my tears.

I Will Hold You In My Heart, Dear Sister, Always and Forever.

—Claudia.

~ ~ ~

My Sister's Hair

I hold onto this dream I had last night of my angel sister Kaylyn. I was focused on her long brown hair, and how it caught the wind as she ran ahead of me. She is so beautiful I thought, her hair so clean, bouncing as she ran, I could see the rays of sunlight dancing through it as I chased from behind.

We fell together as I caught her, laughing, silly young girls of ten and twelve tumbling together onto the grass. It was a beautiful memory of the love between sisters and the innocence of those precious young years.

Then it all began to fade. The dream changed as dreams do, shifting and drifting into something else entirely.

I was watching Kay from a distance, much older now, possibly in her late seventies. She was getting ready for a formal portrait, a classic sitting pose, one hand on top of the other, and in this older version of her, she wore salt-and-peppered grey hair.

At first, I didn't understand seeing her this way, as she had passed in her early fifties, her hair still a rich dark-brown; and she had always told me it would stay that lovely dark brown, even if she had to color it every week to keep it that way. We had laughed about this before, as I confidently wore my crown of silver grey; but not Kaylyn, she thought it would make her look and feel old and said no one would ever see her that way.

BUT I DID, in my dream last night, I saw her hair in peppered grey. Her face had slimmed and her hair had deep streaks of it among dark-brown strands. She was so radiant and pretty, her face still so sweet and kind. The display of years only brought attention to her smile and happy countenance. She was poised and lovely.

I woke feeling so glad that I told her of my love for her when she was still alive and what she meant to me, because we had let many of the years of different lifestyles hold us apart. Now, all fixed and forgotten, only the love remains.

How clever you are little sister, relaying the multitude of our years together through visuals, like hair color and sisterly secrets.

Thank you my sweet sister for coming into my dreams and reminding me of our friendship and our love for one another.

My little sister, my only sister, thank you for sharing your grey hair with me, too! It was for my eyes only, and I know it.

~ ~ ~

A Face in the Crowd

My sister Kaylyn has been instrumental in honing my skills in communication with the Other Side. This is so much her personality of helpfulness, and I am beholden to her, my beautiful loving earthly sister and the patient teacher and guide she is to me now.

I was having a particularly rough day a few months after my mother passed and was praying for a visit from her soon. I wanted to know she was all right. That evening, I had a rather mundane dream.

I was sitting on the ground outside of a shop, working on an antique chair. It was covered in sticky blue-painters tape, and I was scraping it, trying to remove it all from the bottom of a chair and ready it for sale.

A crowd began to gather outside the shop, forming a line, waiting for the doors to open for a big sale. I wasn't paying much attention to them, as I was focused and busy in my restoration work.

At one point, I took repose from my work and noticed the line was getting pretty long. I glanced at the faceless people in the crowd and saw the most beautiful of faces leaning out from behind all of the others. This face was surrounded by a warm golden circle of light, and I recognized it immediately—it was my sister's face—*Kaylyn!* She was beaming at me, with the happiest look of recognition of me, too. She never moved from the line. She just stood there offering the most beautiful smile, my sister's smile, amplified a million times in golden sunshine, smiling at me until I woke.

My sister's smile! She had come in our mother's stead, as this was the way of my helpful loving sister, to let me know that all was OK.

I wondered later if the line represented that I would have to wait a bit for a visit with my mother. Possibly she was not yet ready.

But my little sister came and gave me a most treasured gift, her bright encouraging smile and a silent message, that all was Ok.

A Visit Over the Kitchen Mixer

A Memorial holiday weekend was coming, and I was busy in the kitchen, washing, chopping, cooking and baking, my thoughts floating, my mind unencumbered.

The oven was still warm as I whipped up cookies in a matter of minutes. I threw the ingredients into the kitchen mixer, a gift I had never realized how much I had wanted. Now, I can't imagine ever baking without it.

This is what I was thinking as I picked up a damp cloth to wipe down the machine. In the midst of the simple chores and the silence of room, I heard the voice of my sister.

"Wow, that's slick! I wish I had looked into getting one of those!"

How does one describe a real voice—audible, yes, but only in my head—a voice and a use of words that are not my own—but I *knew*. I instantly recognized Kay, as if she were standing right next to me.

Impossible right? I mean, she was gone—passed, crossed over— she had died.

I giggled at myself and answered her out loud, "I know, right, it's so fast!"

The exchange was so easy, no burning bush, grieving tears or midnight dreams. My sister had found a "crack" in the ease of my mind that morning while I baked and opened the simple sisterly exchange through a seemingly mundane task.

In my heart this conversation was real; nevertheless, I set about to confirm it as best I could. I knew that my sister had enjoyed baking—especially cookies, and I didn't think she had owned a kitchen mixer but I wanted to be sure.

I called her daughter Katie. "Did she have one, or had she ever talked about or asked for one?"

She confirmed that, no, Kay did not have a mixer. "To the best of my knowledge, I can't remember her ever talking about one." I felt this was my confirmation that I had indeed heard Kay, and spent the next few moments thinking how much she would have loved using this machine, too, but would never get the chance.

I thought that was the end of this beautiful story, a lucky encounter, an exchange from beyond, but that was not the case. That evening, as I sat with pen in hand to write in my journal, I suddenly realized there was so much more. The sweetest of synchronicities actually had taken place.

As I wrote the date at the top of the page, I remembered—*Oh, how could I have forgotten this date!*

Kay had passed three years ago today. I was so busy with the process of living and all the day-to-day stuff that I had forgotten this day. I had not found myself watching the dreaded date creep ever closer on the calendar, and then weep over the loss of her. Instead, today while I was busy in my kitchen, my mind at ease—and for that precious moment in time, a crack in thought, a thinning in the veil of separation of our worlds—she came. She was there with me, and I heard her. We spent fun time together in the kitchen—just as she would have liked me to remember her, easily conversing as we always had as sisters, and making warm cookies together.

~ ~ ~

~ ~ ~

Your uniqueness is your value,
and your value is your contribution to the journey

~ ~ ~

14

Service

~ ~ ~

A Whisper of Service

I was working hard in my backyard garden one afternoon, heaving rocks and bags of dirt and mulch, creating a beautiful spot to sit and appreciate during my down time—of which there had never seemed to be enough, since when I did have down time, I was working hard to create "the spot" where I would someday have enough time to really appreciate it. I seemed to be creating the proverbial rolling a boulder uphill scenario.

The query of fleeting time is nothing new. We have all wished for more of it as we begin to notice the sand in the hourglass running out.

At fifty-seven years of age, I looked around at the beautiful garden I had spent years and untold hours creating, mostly for myself. As I marveled at it, catching my breath and wiping the sweat from my brow, I heard something. It was a whisper in my left ear.

I turned to look. There was no one there; I was alone in my garden.

As clear as a bell, I had heard it. A voice. It was soft and gentle enough to be called a whisper, yet it carried weight—and it was audible: *"Service."* One word, that was all...*Service.*

I touched my ear immediately upon hearing it's rendering, and I knew it was meant for me. The voice was from a helper, a guide, a teacher, and this single word spoke volumes. I had been working hard, for myself, and it was time to make some changes in my life.

This was not an instantaneous transition. I thought long and hard about what exactly the voice had meant, and what it wanted me to do. Yes, I kind of reveled in the thought that I had indeed heard a *voice.* I mean, *Wow! Me? I'm just ordinary me.*

But I had heard it—and I *knew* I had something to offer.

Over the next few weeks, I tallied my best attributes, talents, and understandings and took those thoughts and ideas on a hike.

The day was beautiful and the trail a perfect place for my mind to wander. So, I let it.

At one point, I met a group of women who had stopped for a break, sipping from water bottles. We struck up a conversation. They were nurses on their day off. I found myself confessing an admiration for their service, and that I had always wanted to go into that profession. I had always admired those who care for the sick and injured.

One nurse asked why I never did. I gave a brief life synopsis. She said, "Why not go for it now? What's holding you back?"

What indeed?

She continued to push me past my comfort zone, until I was feeling like I was defending myself. But you know—I'm glad she didn't let me get away with claiming it was now about my age, health, time, or money issues. She seemed to have an answer to any and all of my self-imposed limitations.

After I left them, and by the time I finished my hike that day, I had made up my mind—to go online and do inquiries about volunteer service. And by the end of the evening, I had chosen "hospice end-of-life service, and signed myself up for an interview.

Having studied near-death experiences for years, I was already comfortable talking about the afterlife.

After six weeks of training, I was set up in the unit' on the sixth floor of the hospital, on Wednesdays. It was called The Bridge.

It didn't take me long to understand the meaning of *bridge:* the between, the in-between, neither here nor there, in-between.

Those days and hours as a life evaporates are the most sacred of times. Each labored breath exhaled holds weight and girth and calories. Its heat contains the moisture of love and pain, anger and happiness. Thought slips into the air around the head of the dying: their childhood, marriage, children, work, or studies. A lifetime of achievements and regrets are all there, like a deck of cards that was dealt and played, hanging in the air above them, as pharmaceutical sleep invades their last bits of time here on earth.

I found myself on The Bridge with three things: a clipboard containing the patient's name and the ailment that was winning the battle, a book of beautiful poetic words I would read aloud to them to share of the wonder of what was to come when they reached the Other Side, and the most important piece, the angel on my shoulder. This angel nudges and guides me to the room and the person who most needs me that day.

Walking down the hall until compelled to stop, I slowly open the curtain around the bed, concerned about intruding on the last piece of this person's privacy. I introduce myself and ask, "May I stay for a while?" I feel it an honor to share this highly personal time with them, and I treat it as such. I will sit and hold a hand, sharing soft caring words for them and the grieving family.

I patiently wait for the moments between sleep, when I can offer a little water, a smile, or a pat on the hand. Many times, I will gain enough trust to explore their fears and regrets and listen while they share their memories. This is the time for a closer look, and a good talk and a chance to put troubles to rest, for good.

This job is the hardest yet most rewarding I have ever had. At the end of a day, I am exhausted, but I leave filled with more than what I started with.

It is true, that each life is a story unto itself, but each ending is unique as well. Although I have witnessed many experiences from the Other Side at the time of crossing over, the following two have really stayed with me:

~ ~ ~

The Sisters Are Here

During my training in the hospice unit, I spent a lot of time with a seasoned volunteer, Nancy. We were talking one afternoon of the many wonderful experiences she'd had with her patients, and shared many stories of beautiful transitions to the Afterlife.

I listened in fascination, as I had just lost my sister a few months before. The following story of sisters moved me so deeply.

Nancy was sitting at the bedside of a woman named Mavis, a sweet old woman who was very close to crossing, though she was still quite lucid and speaking. As they talked, a beautiful warm smile came across Mavis's face and she gazed past Nancy as if she were looking through her.

Nancy turned and looked behind her, taking a quick inventory of the room. No one else was there. After a few moments of watching, Mavis's face lit up, so Nancy leaned forward and tried to look from the old woman's vantage point.

She still saw nothing, so she asked in a playful tone, "Mavis, what are you looking at?"

It took a minute for Mavis to reply, her gaze still fixed. Then with excitement in her voice, she said, "The sisters are here!"

Nancy looked around the room again and still saw no one. She scooted her chair closer to Mavis and leaned in, the playfulness in her voice subsided, and now in a more serious tone she asked "Your sisters are here with us now?"

"Oh, yes," Mavis said in a sweet and happy tone "There are three sisters here," she paused only briefly before adding, "two of them are mine—but one of them is yours."

Nancy immediately straightened in her chair, caught off guard with this proclamation.

Mavis continued. "Your Catherine is here with *my* sisters!"

Nancy sat in stunned silence. How did a patient she had never met or even spoken to before know that she had a sister Catherine? How could she know that Catherine had indeed passed away, many years ago?

A great many emotions were running through Nancy's mind, and she had to fight to keep her composure in front of her patient. "*But,*" she thought, "*Could her sister really be here right now?*"

In a softened voice, with both curiosity and uncertainty, she asked Mavis, "What is my sister doing? Is she saying anything?"

There was a long pause, as Mavis was beginning to tire, her eyelids were growing heavy. But just before she closed them she answered, "She's smiling at you."

~ ~ ~

Harold

As I walked down the hall of the hospice unit, I read off the names of the patients who are here today, and check their room numbers to see if they had any special-needs requests.

I am there as a representative of "Friends in Faith," as a non-denominational spiritual advisor. I continue walking—until I feel that certain nudge to stop. This morning, it was in front of Harold's room. Harold was an older gentleman about sixty-years-old. He was so emaciated and skinny that I don't think he weighed more than seventy pounds.

As I entered the room, his arms were flailing about in the air and he was distressed. This is normal as one grows close to the end. But he was mumbling. I believed he was asking for water, so I found a lollypop sponge and wet it just enough to moisten his lips and mouth; which is about all a patient in this state can handle. I repeated dipping the sponge into water, then putting it into his mouth, giving him comfort, as lovingly and mindfully as possible.

But his thirst was not quenched by this act. His mouth was opened wide; his tongue was weathered and dry, like a thirsty riverbed with deep canyon crevices.

I filled a straw with water and held it for him. His mouth reached out as lips surrounded the straw like a baby bird. Then I lifted my finger from the straw's top to release water onto his dry tongue. I repeated this several times.

His eyes became more vivid with each small drink, and he reached his arms out toward me, his hands signaling for more, more, more, and patiently, I continued to oblige.

As the day moved on, I stayed next to him. A new distress was his sheets—he didn't want them, as even the weight and heat of the sheet was a discomfort. He pulled at it, exposing the frailty of what was left of his little body, which was covered with bruises. Harold had been through many blood transfusions recently. His legs were almost a deep navy blue, a solid bruise from the knees down. His body showed the scars of a long intense battle he had been fighting, so long it seemed that he would soon finally surrender to it.

I kept talking to him. He was softly mumbling, though his words were inaudible. Talking on for both of us, I asked him if he would like me to read to him, knowing he could not answer. I chose a book I often read to male patients, *"Voyage of Purpose"* by David Bennett, about the author's actual drowning incident during an intense ocean storm when he had worked as a naval engineer. Tossed from a zodiac boat, he had drowned—then returned from the dead. It is a beautiful accounting of the *life-after-life*, and a comfort to many patients facing their own inevitable adventure.

I held Harold's hand as I read. He was finally calming down. After a while, his family entered the room. His wife and daughter introduced themselves and asked me to please continue to read, and I was happy to oblige.

I noticed they stayed across the room from Harold and felt that although they were physically there, they weren't really connecting to him. They smiled at me as I read, and watched Harold from a comfortable distance. He stared at the ceiling as I read, continually mumbling something, and I wished I could interpret his words.

I remained with them as the afternoon passed, though I sensed that his family was holding back. I tried to engage them. I asked whom

Harold might be speaking to - his parents or siblings who passed?

"Both," they echoed, in a simple one word exchange.

"Have you told him it would be alright for him to go?" "Will *you* be alright?"

"The grandchildren have already said their goodbyes," the daughter said.

Her answer left me with feeling of a need to dig deeper. "Can you think of anything between you all that has been left unsaid?"

A strange look came upon both their faces, and silence. After a few awkward moments, the daughter came over to me with a picture of a much younger man in uniform. Attached to the frame were many medals. Clearly Harold was a highly decorated serviceman, a lifetime of achievements that were secured under the glass—despite the room filled with distant relations.

As I looked at the collection of ribbons and medals, I said, "Wow, quite an achiever wasn't he, I can see many years of service here."

His daughter almost snorted at that and said, "Yeah, I guess he was. Yes" quickly adding," he was a real man's man, a type A personality, a real 'gotta get it done' and do it '*my* way' kind of guy."

Her tone spoke volumes. There was clearly a rift between father and daughter. The mother seemed caught in the middle, a position she had held for many years. Pain skirted across her face as she looked toward their daughter, and then took a seat across the room again.

I sat quietly, summing up the situation.

Then Harold tried to speak again, an inaudible mumbling as he stared ahead of him, but he reached for my hand and I looked to where he was looking. I wanted to see what he was seeing, but the veil was lifting only for him.

A few moments later, Harold let go of my hand, his arm outstretched, his hand in a fist. He began to knock in the air before him. *Knock-Knock....Knock-Knock...* It was a poignant beautiful moment and tears rolled down all of our cheeks.

We watched him in silence as he knocked, making several attempts before he dropped his arm in frustration. My heart was breaking and I had to speak up now, and I turned to his family. "I hope you don't mind me saying this, but clearly Harold is still fighting with all of his might. Though it seems it is long past the time for him to go, what is left of his frail body is still holding on. I'm going to leave you now, but before I do, I would like to tell you that if there are words that need to be said, if you are holding anything back, I feel strongly that he can hear you. If you need to yell or talk of disappointments in him, it is better to speak now than to hold it all in and regret it later. Please know that as he is seeing into his future on the Other Side. He can see his faults and misgivings. In his ramblings, he could be asking for your forgiveness before his journey continues, and that forgiveness is only yours to give. Talk to him now and settle the score, if only just to make yourself feel better after this day is over."

I took Harold's hand for a final squeeze, smiled at his family, and took my leave.

It had been a long day and I was too tired to cook, so my husband took us out to dinner. I had made a point not to take my work home with me but this evening I kept thinking about Harold, wondering if he had passed yet, and I mentioned my concerns.

Later that evening as I readied myself for bed, I thought of Harold again, and as I lay there in the dark, I received a flash—a bright, brilliant vision as clear as day. It was of a man in a wheelchair being wheeled outdoors. He was leaving the hospital. I knew it was Harold. He was dressed in full uniform, medals and all, and he looked a hundred pounds heavier and so much healthier!

I knew right then and there that he had passed on and said aloud, "Oh, Harold!" I was so happy for him and for his continuing adventure. I smiled brightly at the sight of him, and his smiling back at me. He raised two fingers to his capped head in a salute of thank you and goodbye.

I barely knew him. Yet, we had shared more than just time. I cried at the kindness he had shown me now to let me know he was passing on, and he was getting better; although his legs were going to take a little more time to heal, he was okay. Perhaps he was even leaving with a lighter heart, after receiving and accepting forgiveness.

"*THANK YOU*, Harold, and *GOODBYE!*" I thought with a full heart. "Goodbye for now, Harold, as you begin your forever journey. Thank you for your kindness in return. I wish you well my new friend."

These two stories are only a smattering of the precious moments of wonder I have witnessed as a hospice volunteer.

I will be forever in gratitude to the pushy nurse who inspired me to search the Internet that day. Above all, a thank you to the voice who cared enough for me to say something before the sand in my own hourglass fell short, a whisper that forever changed my life with the simplicity of a single word, *"Service."*

~ ~ ~

Floating Kleenex

This summer, I lost my mother.

After almost a month since the hospitalization of my sweet mother Lillian, together she and I faced the dissolving hope that the mountain she had been climbing would ever level off. There would be no summit or personal flag planted at the top in celebration of her returning good health. The boulder she had been pushing uphill for the last few years was beginning to slip and gravity would soon take over into an unrelenting spiral downward.

My job throughout her stay in the hospital was the fulfillment of an unspoken contract: I was to remain at her side and witness the decline, the "hard fight" of her will and resilience as her ability to bounce back was fading into the sunset.

I stayed day and night to assist in what remained of her independence, an oxymoron I know but the trust between us was deeply set and I was happy in my duty of guarding her dignity and the remaining decorum of modesty throughout the bed-bathing and bed-panning. She had handed over to me the trust of what was best to do and what she could no longer do solely. She looked to me whenever the doctor came into the room, as she could no longer listen to the advice of the next steps or treatments that could be ordered. We were in varying stages of resignation to the inevitable.

One night in the dark, the night before her passing, as I lay in the familiar padded nook below the window, contemplating the day's events, I had a clear vision.

I was used to a familiar routine of my mother's left hand clutching the hospital tissue box, while her right hand pulled out a folded fresh tissue. She would bring the tissue to her mouth to cough; then she would drop the used tissue to the floor to be collected later as garbage.

This motion had gone on for weeks, the swooshing sound of the tissue being pulled out of the box, followed by the coughing jag, then the soft drop of the balled up soiled tissue to the floor. I had heard it day and night, and I didn't have to rise to look and see what these noises meant. I knew them by heart...

...SWOOSH, COUGH...COUGH... COOUUGHH...DROP.

The vision tonight showed me an entirely different scene: The neatly folded tissue pulled from the box did not drop softly to the floor as she released it. Instead, this time, the tissue defied gravity *and* floated up toward the ceiling. It was the softest of motions, lifting upward like a silent white dove—and I knew I had just received a sign, a gentle certainty that her time was coming to an end, that she would soon be rising out of the restrictive box that had housed her soul.

The rest of the story holds the personal acts and decisions made about anxiety-reducing doses of morphine and the doubts that arise after those decisions are made. I could not help but second-guess everything afterwards. Had I done enough? Had I eased her pain? Was there another treatment I should have tried before letting her go?

In the middle of my grief, then loss, these doubts were tangible. But now I am comforted in the answer to those questions, and I take much comfort in the vision I was gifted the night before her passing, the beautiful message sent to me of her upcoming release, in the form of a soft white tissue floating toward the sky.

~ ~ ~

A Completed Mother and Daughter Contract

After my beloved mother Lillian was no longer here with me, I couldn't help but reflect on my role in her care during her decline in those final weeks in the hospital. Had I made the right decisions? Was she on the right medications? What about possible surgeries or therapies? Were there further treatments I should have looked into, perhaps extend the inevitable? Had I done enough?

These agonizing questions in my grief and loss weighed heavily on me, not from the loved one who is now at peace but from my human frailty, my doubt.

I spent months silently wondering about her care, until one night, I was with her in a dream.

I was caring for her again, but this time I was given the opportunity to step outside myself and watch myself and the way I had treated her those last remaining months.

The dream was a gift of release of my anguish-filled questions. I woke proud of the love I had exhibited, including flossing and brushing her teeth, and putting lotion on her feet and polishing her toenails. I was proud of her too, as she learned to let go of her own independence. The tables had truly turned.

In the dream, I was shown that these acts were a contractual agreement made long before either of our births. This experience between us was a chance for me to repay the motherly love and care she had always given to me.

As I watched myself with her in those final weeks, I realized I had offered her my very best. I had paid it forward and given love and patience back to her.

I woke knowing that the contract between us was accomplished and was now being released. I watched as the signed document lifted upward, and then disappeared. It had been a real and physical thing, and I was grateful for it, for all of it. We had been given many opportunities to serve each other, and appreciated the years we had to share, before we were to say farewell.

~ ~ ~

15

Synchronicity & Coincidence

Coincidence is Gods way of remaining anonymous
—Albert Einstein

~ ~ ~

Black Elk Speaks

My Son Jesse has always had an enthusiasm for the history of the American Indian. We are proud descendants of the Catawba Nation, but have only found fragments of their recorded history. Jesse supplements his curiosity with research of the histories of all Native tribes.

We are both fervent readers, and I have found a treasure trove of used books at second-hand outlets and donation-type stores. One morning I had purchased a bag full of books on various topics, and in a phone conversation with Jesse a few hours later, I asked him to stop by for lunch.

When he arrived, he told me about a book he was reading, how much he was enjoying its message and he wanted me to read it when he finished it. As he continued talking about it, I walked over to the bag of books I had just purchased, remembering one that had caught my eye about Indians. *As* he was telling me the title of his book, I was pulling my book out, turning it over to reveal the title, and as Jesse said "Black Elk Speaks" so did the bold letters on the cover of the book—*Black Elk Speaks.*

We both started laughing at the synchronicity of this, but later that day it proved to be more than one time case of coincidence.

That afternoon someone posted in one of my Facebook groups about a great book they were reading. Yes, *Black Elk Speaks!* I couldn't believe that it had popped up again, in the very same day. I decided I had to Google the book's title, and try to figure out the mystery of this book.

This book was originally published in 1932, with only a few more publish dates in the 1970s and 1980s. This was not a new book and did not have a huge following—but now seems to be acquiring a new audience. Apparently we need to hear what Black Elk has to say.

~ ~ ~

In Honor of Jeanette

The week had been a long emotional rollercoaster of loss, and now I was sitting in a church gymnasium with family, eating ham and funeral potatoes. We were gathered to cherish our memories of my sweet cousin Jeanette.

Across the table from me were people I hardly know anymore—they are the offspring of my beloved aunt Bev, Nona and Loy Dece. These Fabulous Women, along with my mother Lillian, made up the Fantastic Four Strong Sisters. My cousins and I are what remain of them now.

My cousins were some of my favorite playmates when we were children. Sitting across from them now, I can say in all certainty that these people really matter to me, even though it might be over twenty years since I last saw some of them.

The stories we shared this day were rich and full, and ignited memories of the small town of American Fork Utah, where we spent so much time together, riding bicycles and walking to the only movie theatre in town by ourselves. We would often use our chore money for a quick trip to the town bakery to buy pink-and-yellow shortbread-and-sugar cookies. I remember carefully rolling the white paper bags that contained our treats around the handlebars of our bikes. We would head to the town library for a good book and an afternoon rest at the park and read treasured tales in the shade under the trees.

My love of books came from that small library and the summers spent in this small town. I realize now how lucky we were to be young there in that place and time, to be so safe and so free. Together, we would run wild without a care in the world, leaving after breakfast and returning home sometime near dusk, when our stomachs told it was time for dinner.

Now we sat across from each other, comparing wrinkles and the silver tones in our hair. We talked of the years gone by so very quickly and a verse from the song *"American Pie"* took a quick run through my head:

> *"Oh, and there we were all in one place, a generation lost in space, with no time left to start again."*

The meaning of these words probably means something entirely different than I was thinking at this time, the song contains a lot of wordy and thought-provoking verses.

It brought me to the Saturday morning television show we watched as kids, *Lost in Space,* a family of astronauts marooned on an unfriendly planet, each episode an example of their bond, working together to survive, with the strength as a family unit against many a diverse creature or evil doing foe.

Today, surrounded by my family unit, we supported each other in loss as we buried one of us—a sister, friend, cousin, and playmate. I thought of Jeanette, and the reunion she must be having now with her mom, dad, aunts, uncles, and grandparents.

The mood was sad. Even so, at this place and time, at this table, sitting on a hard, metal folding-chair in a noisy church gymnasium, I was surrounded by my cousins, and I was having a really good time. I wondered, "Was it inappropriate to be enjoying myself, here, now?"

At the cemetery, we walked by the gravestones that held our families' chiseled names and important dates—though I did not believe they were there, at the cemetery—not this big loving family. They were at a great party on the Other Side, a room full of them, their arms outstretched and ready to embrace Jeanette in a heavenly welcome home, the love remembered and Jeanette would be bathed in its warmth.

I could not keep the smile off my face, for I was among my kin, the blood of my beautiful grandmother Anna Mildred Hall Strong. I leaned on my Cousin Calvin's shoulder as we recalled our birthday nights at the rodeo together, and our experiences in the comfort of Grandma's house, built close enough to the railroad tracks to feel the powerful vibration. We would fall asleep to the night train's whistle; all of these childhood memories are a part of who I am.

My cousin Rod is a talented musician and piano player, and I appreciated an opportunity to have a good long talk with him. We shared our personal beliefs of the Afterlife, discovering that we weren't so far apart in our thoughts of what comes next.

Across the table, my cousin DeAnna looked and sounded so much like her mother, Loy Dece. It was comforting, as if my Aunt Dece were in the room with us, but I was sure that she was busy at a table on the Other Side—the table that seats all who had gone before. A table for all those who wait patiently for us to join them there, and today they welcomed Jeanette home.

I honestly don't feel that Jeanette would have minded my smiles on this sad day, as all of her family and cousins came together in celebration of *her*. We shed tears of the physical loss of her but we also felt an underlining joy that she was done now, finished with the intangible question of, what was my life's mission?

She has accomplished hers and is now truly home and surrounded by so many who love her. I am not quite ready for that party yet myself, but I do look forward to it, someday.

The time came for us to leave each other, for who knows how many years, or for the occasion that would bring us all together again.

I got into my car to go home, driving down the once-familiar main street, and I noticed how much it had changed—we had all grown up, including the small town of my memories. I drove in silence, reflecting on the day's events, and I entered the freeway ramp before turning on the radio and disturbing the air around my thoughts. I could not believe it as a familiar song began to play. The synchronicity of it still gives me chills. I turned up the volume of the speaker and enveloped myself in the message, a love note from Jeanette on this special day of celebrating her life, and I began to sing out loud:

> "Bye Bye Miss American Pie,
> Drove my Chevy to the levy but the levy was dry,
> And them good ole boys were drinkin' whiskey and rye
> Singing this'll be the day that I die..."

—Don McLean

Thank you, Jeanette, for the fun we had in the years of our youth, and for bringing us all together again in a gathering of love and reflection. I will think of you every time I hear this song, remembering a synchronistic moment we shared, and I will sing along with it again and again, in memory of you.

Love You—your cousin, Claudia.

Universal Support

This story of synchronicities actually started about a week ago. I had spent several weeks gathering and tweaking my journal stories, keeping the ones I thought would make a pretty good book. I was taking a momentary break from this work when I noticed a Facebook post by a friend, and author, Windy Rose Williams. It spoke directly to what I was going through. Since I was the only one so far to LIKE the post, I truly felt it was a message meant for me:

*"Push beyond yourself today. Write about
something that scares you."*

In the comment section, I replied, "Thank you for posting this today. This little push has helped me more than you will ever know."

I'd had a vision a few weeks before, of my guide standing in front of me, putting a computer into my arms, in an effort to help me get started with shaping my stories into a book. So, I've been nudged.

Then I found a story written about my sister, one I had been looking for. For some reason, it wasn't in the documents section where I store my work; so I'd been putting off adding it because I would have to type it again, a seemingly time-consuming task.

I began to dig in to it, reading and copying the words, but I began to feel the original story wasn't finished, that perhaps I was being forced to take a good look at it again. I had a dinner engagement I needed to get ready for, so I left the unfinished sister story looming on the screen. I'd let it simmer and come back to it later.

But I did not come back to it later. The night passed.

The morning came, and I lazily slugged around in my robe. After a second cup of coffee, I opened my I-pad and began to scroll through my personal emails, then moved on to Facebook. I noticed a throwback message waiting for my approval—from 2014. It was a story I had shared about the loss of my sister and a directional sign she had given to me: the story now sitting on my computer screen this very minute. "Whooh!" I shared this exciting happenstance with my husband who also noted "the synchronicity of this is amazing."

But it didn't stop there. As I basked in the serendipity of this event, I scrolled down a few more posts—then caught myself staring in astonishment. A picture of ascending steps made of stone—almost the exact replica of a picture I had printed out and placed in the front of the binder of my gathered materials that I was now calling my book. Oh, my!

I had printed this makeshift cover weeks ago as something

physical, that I could see and feel as a projected finish line—it would be a reminder that I could and would cross it! I *would* finish my book.

I ran now to get the binder. I held it in my hands and looked at the picture I had chosen. I was equally astounded by the words affixed to the picture, on both my copy *and* the Facebook message:

> There will be always being rocks in the road in front of us. They will be stumbling blocks or stepping-stones. It all depends on how we use them.

I felt an extra push—and I *knew* this book I was writing was bigger than me. I also knew that, in the writing of it, I was probably going to stumble a little—but now I was going to add bigger and deeper topics, even if they scared me a little, because now I knew for sure, that the Universe has my back.

~ ~ ~

~ ~ ~

When You Find Yourself Standing In Your Own Way,
Step Aside and Let God Walk In

~ ~ ~

16

Signs & Direction

~ ~ ~

Arrows in the Asphalt Jungle

In the beginning of my personal journey of awakening and enlightenment, I had several dreams of uncertainty and angst, when I was questioning if there was really a *path* and was I traveling in the "right" direction?

In one such dream, I found myself alone in a huge asphalt parking lot, surrounded by varying heights of walls wrapped in chain-linked fencing. I was roaming about in darkness, lost and trying to find my way out of a constructed maze of steel and concrete.

As I walked in this maze, I saw many gates—most were closed and bolted—but some were open just enough for me to squeeze through them. It would take a great deal of walking before discovering another gate and I could not tell if it would be opened to me or bolted closed until I was right upon it.

This fencing went on for miles and miles, so I wearily stopped to collect myself. I needed a decisive plan of action.

Then I found myself standing in front of two gates, one off to my right, the other straight ahead in front of me, and this time, both were opened. *I could really use some kind of guidance*, I thought.

As I stood there taking stock of my predicament and unsure of the way I should go, a large sign came into view, I mean a really big sign, right in front of the opened gate directly in front of me. It was twice the size of me and I had to crank my neck to see the top of its rectangular shape.

It was a white light in the surrounding darkness, and in the middle of the sign was a bold red arrow pointing exactly straight ahead.

So, I gathered myself up, took a deep breath, and walked straight ahead, taking this as a clear *sign* that I should just keep working my way forward—and that, when in doubt, I should stop and ponder the situation and know that if I ask for help and direction it will be offered.

~~~

Stones Along the Road and Other Signs

Walking trails in Colorado Springs, I was near the Air Force Academy on a nicely groomed trail along the frontage road from Monument to Pueblo, a more than fifty-mile trek if you just keep going. This trail was close to home and I could be there within minutes, whenever I wanted a place to go deep into thought.

I'm good for walking a few miles a day, mixing up where I start and end, leaving my car on either end, going so far, then turning around, forcing myself to venture a little further each time. I walk alone; except for two walking sticks I've named Bobbie and Weavie. I've grown accustomed to the click-click-click they make as they hit the ground beside my feet, creating a rhythmic lullaby that allows my mind to wander freely in harmonic bliss.

Talking to my spirit guide as I walk, I crave to actually see him. I feel his companionship and have never doubted he is there. As I walk, I use the stillness to ask him about my proper path in this world, and am I on it? Am I doing okay? I have heard his soft whisper of guidance every now and then, such as when I heard the word *"Service"* whispered into my ear, and also the word *"Trust."* This day I really pushed for something more; I wanted something visual, and I had been asking for it without really noticing what I was already receiving...

White Butterfly

As I walked, I thought back to hikes in the woods and mountains I had taken before. On one hike a white butterfly had flittered alongside me; I took note that it was behaving in a peculiar fashion, staying with me for quite some time. I kept on walking; afraid that if I stopped it would fly away. I did my best to watch it in my peripheral vision, and managed to notice it had large circular markings on its wings that were the whitest of white.

Eventually, after some time, it did fly away—but not before it flew in front of me and seemed to hold still in place just a few feet from my face, before it flew into the bush on the side of the trail.

White Jeep

A few days later I was deep into a walk on another trail, we were camping, and I had hiked *almost* two hours uphill; the downhill would be faster but I was a long way from camp when I noticed clouds gathering overhead. I knew I was in for a wet afternoon but I kept going, wanting to reach a certain plateau or at least the two-hour mark before turning around.

I hadn't seen anyone or any cars up here in the previous days of hiking, but today the sky turned black, and I was fighting my better instincts to go back to camp. Eyes to the sky, I kept going, pushing— when I received what felt like a sign from my guide: a white Jeep appeared from a sister trail ahead and was coming down toward me. It crept along until it was directly at my side. It passed by so slowly I felt compelled to look into the windows, but all I saw was my own reflection in the dark glass. *Why I was giving it so much attention? I wondered. Why did I even care?* But I did.

The Jeep passed me by with no neighborly wave or a "are you doing all right?" It was heading downward, off the mountain. No words were exchanged, but I felt there had been a message for me in our passing. I said aloud, *"Okay, I hear you,"* turned around, and headed right back to camp.

I arrived wet—but I had missed a huge lightning storm that started immediately after my safe return. Hmmm.

White Bird

Another day I was hiking an awesome trail beside the railroad tracks. I love to feel the earth shaking beneath my feet and the vibrations in the air as it rumbles near then passes. I always wave to both the engineer and caboose. Sometimes, I get a wave back.

This day was warm and beautiful and I felt a strong connection to everything around me. I giggled when I noticed a small white bird playing a game of dodge a few paces in front of me. It would fly past me into the woods about knee high on the side of the trail, then in front of me again to the other side of the trail. I enjoyed watching it dart back and forth.

Then a thought made me stop in my tracks: *white butterfly, white Jeep, white bird.* Hmm. I'm no Columbo, but this seemed like a pattern—showing up when I asked to see my guide as I walked. In a playful way, I was getting what I asked for—he was showing himself to me in his own mischievous way—and I finally got it.

Stones Along the Road

Back to the day on the trail near the Air Force Academy, I was asking for yet another miracle—not in a "prove it" kind of way—just for the love of the interaction with Spirit, which is a natural high.

I have an open mind and pay attention to everything around me. I listen, because these quiet walks are the perfect time to "receive" guidance.

So, again, I asked to see my guide—and I heard within, *"What can you give as you wait to receive?"*

Hmmm. I was already receiving so much. What could I give back—right here, right now—that would help another?

I thought about the way that I look for *signs,* the acknowledgements that I am on the right path. Perhaps there was someone walking this trail after me asking the same things? Is there a God? Am I on the right path? Would God give me a sign that I am loved or even heard?

The answer instantly came to me as I looked down upon this well-groomed trail of hardened dirt: a small black stone on the path at the toe of my shoe. I stooped to pick it up and knew that I could be a foot-soldier of God. Right now, today, I could leave a message for someone who needed a sign, a communication from his or her guide, as I had sought so many times before.

I held the small black stone as I walked. It was smooth and well worn and I rubbed it between my fingers—until I came to a wooden bench along the side of the trail. I left it there on the arm of the bench, taking a brief moment to add my intent that it reach someone with a question here on this trail, that it would provide an answer for him or her, a smile, a hug, that Yes, they were being heard.

As I continued walking, I came upon another black stone and picked it up. The groomed trail did not provide many, so each stone felt special in its own right. I filled my pockets with them as I continued, looking for the right places to set them, such as at a fence post or trail sign, so another might see them as inspiration.

I looked for a good spot to leave each stone, a piece of God left for someone in doubt, a hug for another seeking-soul. I found that as soon as I gave one stone away, I would soon find another in its stead. The miles spent walking melted into a blissful joy. I had forgotten about receiving; I was busy giving, my heart thinking of others' needs, and the hope that my little present would be accepted for it's pure intent and purpose.

White Stones

After a while, I came to a bridge with a narrow entrance that I almost had to squeeze through to get to the other side. As I crossed this bridge, I noticed a smooth wooden post. It had a flat-cut top and was a bit taller than me. I might never have noticed it if I hadn't really looked—but I felt *prompted* to look.

I thought briefly that perhaps I would leave a stone here when, to my amazement, I discovered there were *already stones there*! I took a step back, and couldn't believe my eyes. They were white stones— which doesn't sound like a big deal; but so far along this well-groomed trail, I had only seen black stones, and only a few of those.

I stood there blinking, a little dumbfounded, and counted them. One, Two Three, Four, *Five White Stones*, placed in a small circle, and I knew they were meant for me! In awe, I stood humbly—because I *knew* that I was loved—I had been heard.

With this simple gesture of circled stones, all of my questions were answered. It was a huge hug. These stones were from my guide, a gift from the one who had sent me the white butterfly, white Jeep, and white bird. I cupped them into my hand; five amazing rough white stones, and cried openly in appreciation of this physical reminder of the love my Heavenly Father has for me, and for the answers He gives us along our way. All that is needed is that we open ourselves to the answers, pay attention, and while we are waiting to receive: *GIVE*.

~ ~ ~

Rolling Uphill

So many story opportunities come to me during my walks in the woods. A few days after I found the five white stones, I was once again on the trail near the Air Force Academy. It was a perfect morning, full of sunshine and blue skies. It was already nine a.m., a late start in mid-July, especially for a two-hour walk.

As I quickened my pace, I noticed *other* rocks on posts, rocks I hadn't placed myself. Someone else was doing this, too! Someone else had the same intent of giving. "Oh, this is so cool," I said aloud as I passed yet another rock on a post. I had walked this trail many times before and never noticed or seen stones on posts. Perhaps I wasn't paying attention.

This made me think about how many of us go through life never really noticing the simple signs and gestures that we are given along the way. How many times had I missed these sweet hellos? Lately, I was definitely noticing them more and more, and I was feeling a surge of waking up, spiritually, and seeing the connection we all have with our God—or Source, as we know it.

Now I was noticing the sense of humor in the signs being sent along the way and that there are signs around us all the time, reminding us that we are loved and we are not out alone without a lifeline or connection. We notice the signs when the time is right, when we really need it.

If we practice being present, living in the now, we notice simple synchronicities and signs *everywhere*. Just because we never saw something before doesn't mean it wasn't always there. This difference of seeing, not just looking, is where this story really begins.

I was into my own head this day, deep in thought about this new perspective on signs along the way. The consistent clicking of Bobbie and Weavie—my walking sticks—helped me to quicken my pace, as I wanted to beat the afternoon heat on my usual two-hour walk. I was navigating a hill when I noticed a larger stone partially buried into the left side of the trail. It was an interesting color and shape and one I would normally stop to pick up, but at today's quickened pace, it was already many steps behind me and I didn't want to stop and turn around to retrieve it. I probably gave it too much thought, after all it's just a rock; but on this well-groomed trail, there were rarely random rocks—that's what makes finding them made them so special. The fact that it was a rare color and shape was the reason it was still on my mind—so I made a mental note of where I had seen it, to remember where to retrieve it on the way back.

I made my turn around point in just short of an hour and began my trek back to the trailhead. About another half hour had passed when I noticed a different kind of runner approaching from the distance, a runner on wheels. As he got closer, I saw that his legs were tied together, atrophied because there was no working muscle left in them. He was maneuvering himself with his arms, the remaining working body parts of his young twenty-something body.

Shortly after our trail "hellos" another wheeled runner came into view. This young man didn't need his legs tied to keep them out of his way; most of his legs from the mid-thigh down were gone. He was using walking sticks, similar to mine, and using them to propel himself forward while seated in the wheelchair, the wheels turning with the push off the poles and the explosive power of his muscular arms. I was amazed at their determination and resilience as they worked themselves up the hill. I wanted to applaud their dedication to not giving up, and I was filled with admiration for them, making a promised to myself to use their fiery will as an example not to take one day or my health for granted ever again.

A few more steps down the hill, I remembered to look for the half-buried stone and was amazed that I actually found it. Because of its unique shape and mix of color, and the extra effort it had taken to obtain it, I decided to keep it as a "special walking stone" for my future walks, a reminder that at over sixty-years of age, I too was a determined soul; I was out here trying, awesome in my own way. I dubbed it "the special stone of awesomeness" and it would serve as my physical reminder, a solid lump in my pocket lest I ever lapse into self-doubt again.

After a few more minutes, I noticed a large dust storm ahead and a car on the trail; how had anyone gotten through the locked gates to the trail, and why? As I watched the SUV coming toward me, I didn't see that another young and handsome disabled veteran was sitting in the dirt, and I was genuinely startled when I almost stumbled upon him.

His demeanor seemed frustrated and mad, he was hunched over and looking downcast, defeated, his wheelchair turned on its side and below him on the trail. The suburban stopped and parked in front of both of us.

I offered a startled, quick hello and continued my stride, but as I walked forward, it just didn't feel right to leave him. Maybe there was something I could do. The man from the suburban was already retrieving the wheelchair and the situation looked handled. I turned around again to leave, but I could not physically make myself walk forward. I was circling, one step forward, turning, then two steps back. I was circling as if caught in some kind of eddy, an air pocket, or a black hole where all forward movement was halted.

I honestly could not walk away—I knew I had to see if I could help—but I wondered if would I embarrass him by asking. I wasn't strong enough to lift him, and I didn't know what to say or do. I just knew I should go back to him and as I turned, I felt a kind of golden bubble envelope me. I felt an instant peace—the struggle within me abated, and I walked toward him with a determined intent.

As I came close to him, I felt the lump in my pocket thud against my thigh. I reached into my pocket and retrieved the uniquely beautiful stone, and I felt no awkwardness the moment I reached his side. The right words and actions flowed easily as I held out the rock to him. "This may look like an ordinary rock, but it is more than it seems. I have found it to be special in its uniqueness. I keep it in my pocket as a physical reminder of my own awesomeness, because sometimes I forget. I feel strongly that it is now meant for you—so that you won't forget your own *awesomeness*."

Using both of my hands, I lovingly rolled the unique white stone into his hand and closed his fingers over it, giving him a firm squeeze. "You are awesome," I said, and turned to walk away.

The driver of the suburban was watching this exchange, and as I walked past him, he whispered to me under his breath, *"You are Awesome, Thank You."* We smiled as our eyes briefly connected in a genuine caring for this young man. Then, the magical golden bubble dissipated and I continued on my way.

I had felt something in the air, something unseen but definitely there. It was guiding the right words to come from inside me, to be given to this anguished and disillusioned young man. Had he been contemplating giving up on more than this trail ride? Did he need these words to give him hope and help him to keep going? Perhaps a tangible reminder of his own uniqueness.

I will never know what happened to this young soldier after our exchange that day, but I do know, in my heart, that I was guided to him and that a seemingly ordinary rock would prove to be an important gift with its own special purpose.

~ ~ ~

17
Forgiveness & Healing

Forgiveness is the fragrance released when the flower is crushed

~ ~ ~

Letting Go of the Ball of Tar

It Is Possible To Let It Go

The act of forgiveness is a tough one, but I am told that it is important that I share my personal experience with it here.

Forgiveness is easily talked about, and much harder to do—but in the process of working toward enlightenment we must actually let go of the heavy weight that otherwise would hold us down—keep us down.

How can we let our light shine if darkness can be found within? It cannot be compartmentalized or stuffed deep enough to become invisible or forgotten. The venomous snake of hatred may rear its ugly head at the most unexpected of times, since it is exhausting work to keep it covered up and coiled tight.

Forgiveness is an act not easily achieved but, for our overall health and spiritual growth, it is the *soul* solution.

I speak from experience, because I had found myself anchored and shackled to the offenses that were placed upon me by someone else. I was *angry* and thought how *unfair* it was that my life was left in tatters while she danced off, seemingly on her merry way. After building layer upon layer of a deliberated betrayal of someone I was calling friend—no apologies had been offered and certainly no remorse was shown after their actions. So why should I forgive them when they were not even sorry?

I didn't think of myself as dwelling on the offense, because my life had moved ahead and I was okay now, really. I actually had found an inner strength in the exercise of mending the broken shards of what remained after the *cruel* and *thoughtless* acts.

Over time, I knew there was still a *black anger* hiding deep within me. I had pushed it ever downward until a casual mention of her name or a place that stirred memories of the unresolved *hurt* left me feeling a *weak* and *helpless* victim in pain and tears.

I grew tired of the weakness that being the victim brought, and I began to fight back—finding a newfound strength in the *rage* that was rising from within the hidden depths of me. This was much better than tears of weakness, I am *unhurtable* now, and I will cease to care.

Hate is a force that is weighted and strong. For me, it had become a physical *ugliness* emerging from within me. I would revel in a kind of joy around the selective times I would release it, the act of spitting out her name in a form of profanity, my eyes squinting, shoulders heaved up in heavy breath.

I could see only red as my mind pushed out the entirety of anything good in my life that had followed since the time she had spent delighting in the *destruction* of it—it can only be held back for so long until I find myself right back there again—and the *ugly* of it was now *ME*.

Was I a victim? *Yes.*

There was no question or hesitation in my answer. *Yes.*

But I began asking myself—did I need to continue empowering the perpetrator, choosing to live in the *muck* and *mire* that was her creation?

What if I could find the same kind of power *in choosing to leave it all behind me?* What if I could enter fully into *lightness*?

Was it even possible? Being a victim had become a part of my story. It had become easy to draw from this inner *anger* whenever I felt *weak* or *vulnerable*. I had begun to rely on it like a shield that could be wrapped around my heart. I had given it importance—but I had to admit—that shield was becoming heavier and more difficult to carry. I was faced with a choice—and because I had a choice, I realized I also had *control*.

I decided to let it go and to *choose* to *forgive*.

I will not attempt to tell anyone that this decision was easy in any way. I worked very hard toward this goal. I created a formal *Forgiveness Ceremony* and every evening for many days I sat in a meditative state. I then spoke aloud, inviting interaction with God, my higher self, and my guides. I offered a *sincere* and *prayerful* invocation, asking for heavenly assistance in letting go of the darkness that was holding me back. I *vowed* my readiness to break the chains of this anchor tied to my soul.

Over the days that followed, I repeated this ceremony on the list I had compiled of people in my life that I felt had *wronged* me. I was sincere enough to include myself on this list, asking for my own *forgiveness* of the wrongs I had perpetrated on others, also for my *insensitivity* or *careless* behavior that might have been a catalyst for someone else's pain.

I worked on the easy ones first. Admittedly, it felt good. In the days that followed, I thought about the action of *forgiveness* and of its *release* being replaced by a *joy* and a feeling of *lightness*, and I planned the next round of apologies to be offered.

As time went on, I added more work to my list. I wanted to let go of the *self-loathing* and the *doubts* I had held, the *guilt* of past mistakes and *foolish* choices.

One night, the words *"Forgive all"* came into my mind. I had forgiven all except for one, the big one. I still wasn't sure she *deserved* it.

Yet, now, I *understood* it was not my place to *judge*. I wasn't finished with being mad, I realized. I continued to wrestle with this one, a mountain I was not yet ready to climb. So I left it for "another" time.

Then a dream came one night, *troubling* dreams of dark caldrons full of *negativity* and bubbling lava and I had also dreamed of her, the object of my *darkest emotions*. I shook myself awake out of the dream, and lay in the darkness in a *troubled* form of *fear*. I was made to know that my spiritual progression was being held back, slowed and halted, and I was the one responsible. I was holding myself back. She no longer had anything to do with it.

I trembled in the darkness and tried to comfort myself away from the dream. I brought my hands up to my face but found no comfort there. I moved my hands to my shoulder and slid them down the length of the arm, past the elbow to my wrist, in a type of squeegee motion; then did the same on the other side.

I was pushing against my skin, trying to etch out the *negativity* from within. Could I rid myself of this *poisonous* venom?

I slid my hands against my legs, my head, my gut, visualizing all the parts of my skin and body being cleansed.

The act was so real in my mind that, as I finished, I could see in my mind's eye that this action of *release* had expelled a large *sticky ball of tar—oily, dark black, mucky and dank*. I saw myself holding a tar baby of sorts. This visual was so real— it was *awful* and *disgusting*.

Where can I put it? I thought, thinking of the clean sheets and blankets around me. It was a *mess*, and I no longer wanted anything to do with the *darkness* and *smite* contained within it. A screen appeared before me, the same screen I had now grown accustomed to seeing whenever being sent a psychic message or vision. A person appeared before me in the form of a living-breathing picture—it was *Her*.

I watched silently as she turned and looked at me directly, opening her mouth wide, exposing a gaping hole of tongue, lips and teeth. I instinctively knew what I was supposed to do. I tossed the *terrible ball of sticky tar* into her mouth to be swallowed whole. It was hers now to carry, and it would reside inside her until she dealt with it and resolved it herself. The *filth* was her creation, and now I had given it all back to her. Now it was her choice how she would deal with it.

There comes a time at the close of our earthly lives, when we have the chance to relive and review acts that we hardly remember. We will have a chance to feel the *gratitude* firsthand for the thoughtful acts we shared and be witness to the times we were *charitable* and cared for others. These acts will render themselves like ripples in a stream.

We will also be more than audience to the pain and destruction we have caused. We will feel this from the perspective of the ones we left in pain, for that is the *truest* of judgments.

To judge is not of God who *loves* and *adores* us *unconditionally.* We will stand in our own form of judgment of our own deeds, feeling more than shame for reckless acts as we watch ourselves in a 360-degree view. We will feel our own actions through those we have *wronged*, as if they were actually *happening to us.*

This is the only judgment—*and it is offered as a gift and not a punishment,* so that we will learn to give *unconditional love* for each other and to ourselves. This is accomplished by our bearing witness to the *hurt* and *pain* we have rendered and in complete contrast to the feeling of *acceptance of warmth and happiness when uplifting others.*

In the end, all is forgiven. God has only love for us—and LOVE is the whole of God, the Source.

We have been given an ability to change course as we reside here on Earth, where *forgiveness* can be achieved and used as a tool toward advancing our *spiritual development.* We do not have to wait until we find ourselves on the Other Side, standing before God in remorse during our review.

There is a choice that we can make in the here and now. We can give ourselves a lighter load to carry, by *forgiving* and *letting go* of the darkness and moving completely *into the light.*

~ ~ ~

Life Is a Multiplicity of Patches

Some Saturday mornings, I am compelled to wake early, just to be by myself before the hustle bustle of the day ahead. I find an easy comfort in snuggling into the familiar worn spots on the couch, under a warm fuzzy blanket, searching the television for a lazy weekend movie. It must tell a graceful story, one that is soft touching, emotional, and deep thinking that will allow me to be fully enveloped. The story must leave just enough room for me to remember my own past loves and talents long pushed away, a safe place on a lazy Saturday morning to bring up the ghosts of my past, and with an appreciation of them. Most importantly, it must leave space and time for tears, the cleansing one needs every once and awhile.

This morning's choice was perfect, and I knew it would be, because it has been the perfect choice many times before: *How to Make an American Quilt,* a history of family, through artful, picturesque hand-sewn quilts passed down for generations.

The characters wind you into their private worlds and the residual effect their choices have had on their lives, weaving a beautiful story of happiness and pain. You know the story—it is called LIFE. And in its living, we all end up with an interesting *story* to tell.

I would like to offer here that you should write your own life's story, jot it down for your children and for future generations. Most of all, though, you should write it for yourself—as an opportunity to revel in the remembrance of your life's joys, pain and trials, and your growth and strengths earned after crossing the threshold of them. Let writing your story be an opportunity to ponder the experience of *you* and your unique signature that will be forever woven into the Universal tapestry.

You have a quilt inside of you, sewn with remnants of colorful fabric pieces that represent all the choices you have made and the chances you have taken, the loves you have won and the losses you have endured. Let the reflection of your life open a closed or tired heart, and to remember how truly magnificent you really are.

Perhaps taking a lazy morning off to reflect on your life every now and again will tempt you into starting a brand new life chapter, or perhaps a leap of faith into offering some needed forgiveness. There are still chances to take, and it is never too late, until it is.

My sincere wish, dear reader, is that you take a contemplative walk through your own garden's path, enjoy a reflective look at your own life's quilt, and discover that it already contains a multiplicity of a colorful patchwork of pieces, and it is beautiful:

New Lovers Look for Perfection
Old Lovers Learn the Art of Sewing Shards Together
And Seeing Beauty in a Multiplicity of Patches

~ ~ ~

I'm Fixing a Hole Where the Rains Came In

I do not mean to idealize the act of forgiveness as an easy fix. There was a time when I knew *hate* on a first-name basis. I held its hand as if it were a friend. It created supercharged adrenaline that pulsed through my veins, giving me a type of caffeinated energy for the day ahead. It ran through me as I trained for marathons. I captured it, using it as a substitute for valuable and needed calories. I found satisfaction and sustenance in hardening the outside appearance of my body. However, there was a point when the adrenaline ran dry and I was forced to look inward and examine my wounds; what I found there was a hurt and needy child.

At about this same time, the Eagles came out with the song "Get Over It," with the words "I'm gonna find your inner child and kick its little ass." Needless to say, the inner child was getting lots of airplay and attention—and I was taking notice.

It took me a lot of effort over a lot of years, but I worked very hard, and in quoting a great proponent of forgiveness and healing, Iyanla VanZant, she states, *"Do the Work"* and I *Did the Work.* Now I know that forgiveness can be a beautiful release from binding shackles.

Recently, I dreamed I was with my son Aaron sometime after he had finished building a beautiful new home where he and his beautiful wife Kate were going to raise their children—my grandchildren—some of my most favorite people in the world.

In the dream, I was at his home—but there was something missing. The roof wasn't finished and heavy rains were setting in. The entirety of the inside of the home was beginning to fill up with mud. I tried to clean up the mess, furiously working to fill and haul out bucket after bucket, but more continued to pour in and I was fighting a losing battle.

I came to the realization that I could not accomplish this task alone. That's when I heard hammering above me on the roof. I looked up to see my ex-husband working hard to help the son he loves, too. Though our past had been filled with much contention, I was very happy to see him and also filled with a strong desire to work with him. There was much to do, and I knew that if we worked together we could fix the hole and clean up the mess, which was having a serious impact on the children and grandchildren we both loved.

As we worked together, we declared a kinship and finished the cleanup with a proclamation that we would proceed in working together on cleaning up our own mess, so to speak.

I have had many dreams of this nature in the last year, of friends and of acquaintances. I have reviewed and revisited many hard-to-look-at situations, and either asked for, or offered, my forgiveness. I've done a lot of cleaning up and learned that as I take on an active spiritual role, much of the old has to be let go of in order to make room for the new.

I am continuing to work toward cleaning up my old messes.

~ ~ ~

~ ~ ~

It is possible to move a mountain
But the task will seem easier...
if you start with the small stones first.

~ ~ ~

Epilogue

*You Must First Look For Something
Before You Can Find It.*

These words came to me last night. They scrolled across my vision while meditating.

I believe it is a universal message—meant both for you, dear reader, and for me—as knowledge is not just handed to us.

If you're curious about a subject, dive into whatever materials you can find about it, join groups whose members pose the same kind of questions you have. Read, pray, meditate, *ASK*. Work on *staying still* just a few extra moments every morning when you wake, and contemplate. Did you receive the answer in your dreams? Did you wake feeling stronger or more attached to a new concept than ever before?

The Universe is willing and ready to provide us with answers, but we must first look for them ourselves. The power and knowledge is already within, waiting to be explored.

Thanks & Appreciation

I have carried this book inside me for a very long time, written in short stories on various scraps of paper or bedside journals, in addition to research through countless media posts and computer document downloads.

~

It was my dearest friend Charlene Daniels who first realized I had a book inside me. She commented on this through a cartoon she sent my way and its message was clear: a gowned patient under the x-ray machine, the doctor saying, "Oh, now I know what is wrong with you. You have a book inside of you."

After forty-plus years of unwavering friendship, she was the one who recognized that, indeed, I was suffering from this special ailment and encouraged me that it was time to get it out.

Thank you, my dearest friend, for your gentle, and occasional not-so-gentle pushes along my path of enlightenment. Also, for your patience on the other end of the phone as you blew new life and insights my way when I found myself stuck. Thank you for all of our years of friendship, as you are my closest confidant and soul sister.

~

Thank you my friend, Charol Messenger, an accomplished writer and award-winning author of many beautiful books. Our finding each other is another serendipitous story. Our friendship was not a simple coincidence. Thank you for guidance.

~

Thank You God for my dear friend and author, Deirdre DeWitt Maltby, for whom I created my own destiny to find and meet her. I was so drawn to her soul. Her NDE and experience with God is so captivatingly real. The light oozes from within her in love and acceptance. There is a beautiful story in our finding one another and I know our spirits have been kindred for eons of time.

~

Thank you to Joan Pearson, my loving mother-in law who told me she loved me long before her son did. Thank you for listening to my unfinished works and stories and for your boundless enthusiasm of them. You moved mountains in amplifying my courage to open up and share them and you helped me to understand that perhaps I did have something to say indeed.

~

I must mention a special Facebook group, lead by the gifted Shannon Johnson. It is one I found myself a part of by accident, believing that there are no accidents. It is a loving and tightly knit family of warmth and kindness and open-minded seekers. It is private and keeps a small membership, but each Stones of Wisdom member is so talented and special to me. Each has contributed to my growing confidence and spiritual growth in their own way.

~

I am grateful to all of my extended friends and family; especially my beautiful children who are making a difference in the world, Sarah, Jesse, Aaron, Eric and Chelsea Rose, and to their well chosen partners Jami, Kate, Miah and Danny, and to my step-daughters, Amber, Kristin and Lynnsie, and to my grandchildren who are life's greatest blessings.

~

I add special mention here to my Son Jesse, for his acceptance of me as we share abstract concepts, and for his unwavering belief in me and what I receive, and forever a beacon of light. Thank you to my son Aaron for the beautiful poetry given me years before this book was even a distant dream, and for allowing it to be shared with the world.

~

A very special thank you to my brother-in-law Curtis Pearson for cover design and artwork, layout and the uncountable hours of long-distance editing. I appreciate your calm demeanor in handling my moments of angst, and worry that this book may never be finished, and especially for your resistance in squelching my artistic license and creating a feeling of simpatico, sincerely, thank you.

~

A heartfelt Thank You My Love to Chris, my husband of over twenty-five years. You have been witness to and most affected by my transformation and growth. You are honest with me when you tell me you don't get all of this stuff, and I can appreciate that, as we all walk at our own pace toward enlightenment. You have grown to accept that I am weird and have tender feelings. You have tried to listen as I shared unexplainable dreams, and accepted the days of my writing stories when you felt I should be working at a "real" job. Your own hard-working ethic has been a good example for me and also has allowed me the freedom to revel in this writing arena for the many months it has taken me to put all of this together and format the book's puzzle pieces into one solid workable piece. After all of our years together, I love you still—and will forevermore.

~

And though they do not require mention, how can I not extend my deepest gratitude to my spiritual guides and angels who accompany me along my way, whisper in my ear, and send me visuals and wise dreams. I am humbled by the love I have felt from them all, especially Click Click, my personal spiritual teacher and friend, thank you for all of the nudges into my spiritual wakefulness.

Recommended Reading

I always appreciate the author's list of recommended materials and who were the greatest influences on their journey. I have found many inspiring works in my years of research, too many to name all here, but I offer the following, as books that changed my entire world and I am confident they will change yours, too.

David Bennett: VOYAGE OF PURPOSE & A VOICE AS OLD AS TIME

Nanci Dannison: BACKWARDS

Mary Deioma: LOVE A TRANSCENDENTAL JOURNEY

Deirdre DeWitt Maltby: WHILE I WAS OUT, and WHISPERS TO THE SOUL

Richard Martini: FLIPSIDE: A TOURIST'S GUIDE ON HOW TO NAVIGATE THE AFTERLIFE and IT'S A WONDERFUL AFTERLIFE and HACKING THE AFTERLIFE

Charol Messenger: HUMANITY 2.0, THE NEW HUMANS: SECOND GENESIS, THE SOUL PATH, YOU 2.0, WINGS OF LIGHT, INTUITION FOR EVERY DAY

Michael Newton: JOURNEY OF SOULS

Paxton Robley: NO TIME FOR KARMA

Made in the USA
San Bernardino, CA
08 June 2020

72902757R00124